Six Healing Sounds

Nurturing

Life

Qigong

六字訣

Simon Blow

First published 2017
Copyright © 2017 Simon Blow

National Library of Australia
Cataloguing-in-Publication data:

Six Healing Sounds – Nurturing Life Qigong

ISBN: 978-0-9873417-4-7

Published by:
Genuine Wisdom Centre
PO Box 446
Summer Hill NSW 2130
Australia
www.genuinewisdomcentre.com

Editing:
Elizabeth Bond
www.whirlybirdwords.com.au

Cover design and layout:
Determind Design
www.determind.com.au

Diagrams:
John Bennetts
www.johnbennettsmusic.com

Disclaimer
The intention of this book is to present information and practices that have been used throughout China for many years. The information offered is according to the author's best knowledge and is to be used by the reader at his or her own discretion and liability. Readers should obtain professional advice where appropriate regarding their health and health practices. The author disclaims all responsibility and liability to any person, arising directly or indirectly from taking or not taking action based upon the information in this publication.

This book is dedicated to

All those seeking harmony and positive change in the world.

If there is light in the heart,
There will be beauty in the person.

If there is beauty in the person,
There will be harmony in the house.

If there is harmony in the house,
There will be order in the nation.

If there is order in the nation,
There will be peace in the world.

Old Chinese Proverb

Based on a Confucius saying

Contents

Acknowledgements

There are many people I would like to thank for helping me to compile and develop this book.

Since I started teaching full-time in 1992, I have taught many classes each week for the general public and within therapeutic communities. I have had the great opportunity to meet many people on their own healing journey and I have been inspired by their stories. I get many ideas and positive feedback from all of the people I meet and from those who have generously shared their own experiences in this book. I'm not sure if we have original ideas or if, when the heart opens and the Qi flows, we are simply all one. Again, thank you.

I would like to thank all who have attended my classes, workshops and residential retreats over the years. Also to those who have travelled to China with me. Without all your help and support I would not have been able to continue on this path.

I would like to thank Elizabeth Bond for proofreading and editing and for bringing this project to life. Thank you John Bennetts for the original photos and drawing adaptations; every diagram is a work of art and Master Zhang Cheng Cheng for the original Chinese writing. Thank you to Mamun Khan and all his team from Determind Design for the layout and design.

We refer to Qigong as an art form. It is a process of refining our internal energy to harmonise with the external energy or environment. It's our own observation of our relationship with everything around us. We are influenced by everything around us; we are one with everything.

About the Author: Simon Blow

A near fatal accident at the age of 19 lead Simon to investigate various methods of healing and rejuvenation, a path he has been following ever since. Simon is a Sydney-based (Australia) master teacher (Laoshi) of the ancient Chinese art of longevity and has been leading regular classes for beginning and continuing students since 1990.

Having travelled the world to learn and explore this ancient art, Simon has received extensive training and certification from many respected sources: Traditional lineage Grand Masters, Traditional Chinese Medical hospitals and Daoist monasteries in China, Buddhist monasteries in Australia, and Hindu ashrams in India. He has been given authority to share these techniques through his teachings and publications.

Simon has received extensive personal training in the Da Yan Wild Goose Qigong from the 28th lineage holder Grand Master, Chen Chuan Gang, and is an initinated student and 29th Generation of this ancient healing art.

He received World Health Organisation certification in medical Qigong clinical practice from the Xiyuan Hospital in Beijing and is a Deputy Secretary of the World Academic Society of Medical Qigong in Beijing. He has also been initiated into Dragon Gate Daoism and given the name 'Xin Si', meaning 'genuine wisdom'.

Simon has spent quality time on many occasions at the Ramana Ashram in Southern India under the sacred mountain of Arunachala, following the self-realisation practices of Sri Ramana Maharishi.

His dedication, compassion and wisdom also make Simon a sought after keynote speaker, workshop and retreat facilitator. By demand he has created a series of Book/DVD sets and guided meditation CDs. He also helped produce CDs for the Sunnatram Forest Monastery, the YWCA Encore program and a series of meditation CDs for children and teenagers.

China holds a special place in Simon's heart. He has had the great fortune to travel to China on many occasions to study Qigong, attend international conferences, tour the sacred mountains and experience the rich culture of the Chinese people. Since 1999 he has been leading unique study tours to China so he could take people to the source and give them the opportunity to experience firsthand this ancient healing practice.

Romanisation of Chinese words

The Genuine Wisdom Centre uses the Pinyin Romanisation system of Chinese to English. Pinyin is a name for the system used to transliterate Chinese words into the Roman alphabet. The use of Pinyin was first adopted in the 1950s by the Chinese government, and it became official in 1979 when it was endorsed by the People's Republic of China.

Pinyin is now standard in the People's Republic of China and in several world organisations, including the United Nations. Pinyin replaces the Wade-Giles and Yale systems.

Some common conversions:

Pinyin	Also spelled as	Pronunciation
Qi	Chi	Chee
Qigong	Chi Kung	Chee Kung
Tai Ji	Tai Chi	Tai Jee
Taijiquan	Tai Chi Chuan	Tai Jee Chuen
Gongfu	Kung Fu	Gong Foo
Dao	Tao	Dao
Daoism	Taoism	Daoism
Dao De Jing	Tao Teh Ching	Dao Teh Ching

The use of Chinese characters in this publication

Chinese writing has been a developing medium for thousands of years and is the oldest continuously used system of writing in the world. It's the foundation of many of the other Asian styles of writing, originating from simple pictures to complex brush strokes with many thousands of individual characters. Since the 1950s, traditional characters which numbered in the tens of thousands, have been simplified to four or five thousand. Even though there are many different dialects spoken in China, including Mandarin and Cantonese, the characters remain the same and their written technique and meaning are taught in all schools across China. The computerised font used for Chinese characters which are used today and in this publication are simplified Chinese. Some of the deeper meaning or essence from the ancient times has been lost in the translation from traditional to simplified characters.

A good example is the word 'Qi' as written in Pinyin or sometimes written as 'Chi', which is used to describe the 'energy of life' or 'life force energy'.

氣 The traditional character for Qi shows a picture of a pot being heated on a fire, or the cooking of rice with steam smouldering from the top as a result of the cooking which relates to the refining process of cultivating the internal energy.

气 The simplified character for Qi only shows the steam rising and is sometimes translated as air or breath, losing the deeper understanding of cultivation or refining.

How to use this book

Traditionally we follow the teacher/master and this balances our energy. The book gives detailed instructions on how to perform the movements and provides additional theory and history to complement the practices. To view videos showing the shape of the movements please visit our YouTube channel **www.youtube.com/simonblowqigong**

It's important to learn from an experienced qualified teacher and to practise regularly to master the movements yourself. Attending regular classes provides consistent practice and refinement and the energy of the group nurtures and supports everyone. It's important not to stray too far from the flock.

Chapter 1
Introduction

Six Healing Sounds
Nurturing Life Qigong

Introduction

The Six Healing Sounds, or 'Liu Zi Jue' as it is called in China, is one of the historical and classical health cultivation practices that has been in use for over 2000 years. Our Ancestors from all cultures in the world have been using their voice as a means of connecting and harmonising our internal world with the external world and becoming one with the self or the divine energy. The ancient Chinese developed the Six Healing Sounds from their own understanding and connection with nature as a way of improving health and promoting healing and longevity.

According to Traditional Chinese Medicine (TCM), the five major organs: heart, spleen, lungs, kidneys and liver, relate to a different Element: fire, earth, metal, water or wood. Each organ also has a specific sound it resonates with; by using this sound in conjunction with the inhaling and exhaling of air, stale Qi can be expelled by creating different internal vibrations and pressures within the organ. When stale Qi is expelled or purged from the affected organ, it is replaced with fresh, clear Qi. This helps to balance and harmonise the emotions which are associated with the organ.

As human beings, we have been on a constant search to find meaning, happiness and fulfilment in our world. In modern life sometimes we tend to be too focused on achieving external goals, or on accumulating material possessions thinking we will become successful or happy. While it's important to be motivated, at an excessive or extreme level this can cause stress and anxiety and can reduce our quality of life. Maintaining a healthy life is about finding balance and harmony within all the aspects of our world as well as within our bodies.

Nurturing Life

An important component of Chinese culture and TCM is the principle of 'Yang Sheng'. 'Yang' translates to 'taking care of', to 'nourish' or 'nurture' and 'Sheng' translates to 'birth' and 'vitality'. Together the words mean to 'nurture or nourish life', to 'foster a state of wellbeing by nurturing mind, body and spirit'. Yang Sheng is a manageable practice for all people, aimed at cultivating health and harmony through daily activities. The focus is on maintaining balance through an awareness of our connection with nature and our environment, our physical bodies and our spirit. Health preservation (instead of disease treatment) is an essential feature of TCM practice and is significantly different to Western medicine, which mainly focuses on disease and illness.

Many of the Yang Sheng principles are outlined in the book Huangdi Neijing or The Yellow Emperor's Internal Canon of Chinese Medicine, which dates back 2500 years. From my own experience studying the Chinese healing arts and travelling to China on many occasions, I have been continually learning from my Chinese teachers and friends about the basic understanding of Yang Sheng: "on why we eat certain foods and how the dishes are arranged and balanced with heating and cooling elements to balance Yin and Yang, how drinking warm green tea cleanses the fats from food and aids in our digestion, to remain calm and not waste our energy and to learn to sit quietly to cultivate the mind and nurture the spirit."

The study and practice of Qigong is a key element of Yang Sheng health cultivation. When we circulate Qi and clear stagnation within our meridians or energy system, this enables our Qi field or aura to increase, allowing us to achieve harmony in mind, body and spirit.

Qigong

The word 'Qigong' is made up of two Chinese characters, 'Qi' and 'Gong'. 'Qi' (Chi) translates to the 'energy of life', the vital energy which flows through the network of meridians in the body and connects with the energy or Qi of the universe. In Japan and Korea it's known as 'Ki' and if studying Yoga the term 'Prana' is used. Most cultures have a similar terminology for life energy. 'Gong' (Kung) is a term which translates to 'work, mastery, skill and training'. The two words therefore translate to 'energy work', 'working with the energy of life' or 'mastering the energy of life'.

氣 功

Qi   Gong

The practices of Qigong date back many thousands of years and the underlying principles and concepts are intertwined with Chinese culture. An older term for these energetic movement and stillness practices that have been used since ancient times is 'Dao Yin', which translates to 'guiding exercises'. The word 'Qigong' has only been used since the 1950s as a way of classifying all of the Qi or energy techniques. It can be categorised into three separate sections; Martial/Sports Qigong, Medical/Healing Qigong and Spiritual/Meditation Qigong and within these sections there are hundreds or even thousands of sub-categories.

Qigong is one of the great treasures of Chinese culture and an integral component of Chinese medical health systems. The understanding and cultivation of Qi is one of the underlying principles of Daoist, Buddhist and Confucius practices, as well as the martial arts. The art of Qigong consists primarily of meditation, relaxation, physical movement, mind-body integration and breathing exercises. There are thousands of different styles and systems practised: done standing, moving, walking, sitting or lying down. Taijiquan or Tai Chi is another popular style.

From ancient times, Qigong was developed as a way of helping improve people's quality of life. When the mind and body come into a state of balance, stress is reduced and there is an increase in health and longevity. This allows us to become naturally in harmony with our environment and the universe.

Six Healing Sounds History

Records of the use of the Six Healing Sounds can be traced back to the Warring State Period (475-221 BC). Legend tells us that Zhuang Zi, an influential Daoist philosopher, mentions the benefits of using the breath and different sounds to dispel excess heat from the body and to harmonise the internal organs and the emotions. A detailed description of the Six Healing Sounds was recorded in *Tai Qing Jin Ye Shen Dan Jing (Great Clarity: Scripture on the Divine Elixirs of Golden Liquid)* written by Yin Chang Sheng Zhenren in the Eastern Han Dynasty (25-220 AD).

It's generally recognised that the Six Healing Sounds were officially recorded in Yang Xing Yan Ming Lu *(Records on Nourishing Character and Prolonging Life)* by Tao Hong Jing (456-536 AD), a leading figure of the Maoshan School of Daoism. This states that Qi circulation can be promoted by inhaling through the nose and exhaling through the mouth. There is one way of inhalation but six ways of exhalation.

The Tong Meng Zhi Guan *(Samatha-Vipasyana or Insight Meditation)* by Buddhist Master Zhiyi also records the benefits of the Six Healing Sounds in treating disease and harmonising the inner body.

In the Tang Dynasty (618-907 AD) Daoist priest and medical expert Sun Si-Miao, who was known as the 'King of Medicine' due to his achievements in advancing Traditional Chinese Medicine, wrote in the *Song of Hygiene* about the Six Healing Sounds:

"The Liver and Spring are classified as Wood Elements; the Xu sound in the spring will brighten the eyes and relieve liver stagnation. The Heart and Summer are classified as Fire Elements; the Ke sound in the summer will relieve fire in the heart. The Lungs and Fall are classified as Metal Elements; the Si sound in the fall will nourish the lungs. The Kidneys and Winter are classified as Water Elements; the Chui sound in the Winter will keep the kidneys at ease. The Xi sound will regulate the Triple Burner and eliminate annoying heat. The Hu sound during the four seasons will assist the assimilation of food by the spleen. It is not necessary to make any noise when you practise."

No physical movements accompanied the practice of the Six Healing Sounds until the Ming Dynasty (1368-1644 AD), when Hu Wenhuan and Gao Lian wrote books on the subject, including basic movements to stimulate the meridian channels associated with the particular element and sound.

Ma Li Tang (1903-1988 AD) was a Doctor of Traditional Chinese Medicine from Beijing, a famous martial artist and a Qigong Grand Master. He promoted and popularised the ancient Six Healing Sounds during the modern wave of Qigong from the 1950s. His influence and dedication has protected and preserved this ancient health cultivation practice. In 2003, the Chinese Administration of Sport with the help of Chinese linguistic experts released a modern version of the Six Healing Sounds, which was widely promoted as Chinese Health Qigong. In 2015, the Shanghai Qigong Research Institute published a detailed book and DVD on the Six Healing Sounds featuring an earlier version from the Ming Dynasty.

The Six Healing Sounds has undergone many adjustments and refinements throughout its long history, with historical figures and many prominent masters and doctors contributing to its assimilation into different spiritual traditions and TCM, all helping to increase the quality of life of all people.

I was first taught the Six Healing Sounds in 1995, when I started assisting Qigong Grand Master Jack Lim who was conducting Qigong workshops in Sydney. I was fortunate to receive quality one on one training on many occasions. Grand Master Jack Lim shared many stories of his own training when he was a student of Grand Master Ma Li Tang in Beijing. I started teaching the Six Healing Sounds to my students in 1997. From 1998 I started travelling to China regularly, attending international Qigong conferences in Beijing and discussed their application and theory with other Qigong practitioners. My Chinese teachers and friends would often coach me on the correct way to position the tongue and hold the mouth when making the sounds to get the correct tone. I have always received positive feedback from students and most seem to feel the organs vibrating and a shift in energy when practising the Six Healing Sounds.

Chapter 2
The Details- how does it work?

Six Healing Sounds
Nurturing Life Qigong

The Details- how does it work?

Emotions and Traditional Chinese Medicine (TCM) Theory

In TCM, the state of the emotions is interpreted differently than in Western medicine.

Anger in TCM is an expression of resentment, frustration and irritability. It is believed anger can be caused by an excess of rich blood which can affect the liver, and when this organ's energy rises to the head it can result in headaches or dizziness. When anger is released from the liver, the virtues of kindness and compassion appear.

The emotion of joy is not elation or happiness, rather it refers to a state of agitation or overexcitement. Associated with the heart, when this emotion is out of balance a person may experience heart palpitations, agitation or insomnia. When this overexcitment is released from the heart, the virtues of acceptance, love, peace and calm emerge.

Worry or over-thinking is a product of excess mental stimulation and can affect the spleen, which results in fatigue, lethargy or difficulty concentrating. When worry is released from the spleen, the virtues of honesty, trust, faith and openness appear.

The lungs are associated with the emotion of grief and unresolved grief may affect a person's Qi (life force) because the lungs are responsible for distributing Qi throughout the body. When this grief or sadness is released from the lungs, the virtues of strength, righteousness, integrity and dignity emerge.

While fear is a normal emotion, if it becomes chronic the kidneys can be affected and their ability to hold Qi may also be disrupted. When this excess fear is released, the virtue of wisdom, perception and self-understanding appear.

All emotions are a normal and healthy aspect of being human. It is only when they become extreme or out of balance that they can lead to ill health and disease. TCM believes the emotions are the most significant internal cause of disease within the body, but also the most easily influenced. With the right attention and treatment, emotions and their corresponding ailments can change.

TCM believes that in relation to health, cause and effect are not linear but circular. This means that the cause of an ailment may be an emotion, but also that an ailment can lead to an emotion. By balancing the organ related to a person's emotional state, the emotion can be balanced and visa versa.

Five Elements and Traditional Chinese Medicine (TCM) Theory

The Huangdi Neijing (Inner Canon of the Yellow Emperor) states that: 'The five Yin organs of the human body produce five kinds of essential Qi, which brings forth joy, anger, grief, worry and fear.' In TCM, the emotion of anger relates to the Wood Element, joy to the Fire Element, worry to the Earth Element, grief to the Metal Element and fear to the Water Element. Each organ also has an association with an Element: the liver with Wood and therefore with anger, the heart with Fire and joy, the spleen with Earth and worry, the lungs with Metal and grief and the kidneys with Water and fear.

Positive emotions are experienced when an organ vibrates at a higher frequency than usual. Negative states manifest when the energy flow is fragmented, stagnant or sluggish. When a person's Qi is negatively affected by a bad diet, poor lifestyle choices, repressed or extreme emotions or a weak constitution, pain, discomfort or illness can develop.

The Six Healing Sounds assists in moving congested Qi and allowing the body to dispel it by giving the internal organs a good 'massage'. When practising, at first a positive state is only experienced for a short time. With regular practice the body's energy system begins to change and eventually vibrates at the higher frequency. This can result in a shift in consciousness and a positive change in our relationship with ourselves and others.

Pronunciation and Variations

There are a few different variations in the pronunciation of the Six Healing Sounds; China is a very large and diverse country with many different dialects spoken. The pronunciation of Chinese characters or writing has varied throughout history and also varies in different geographical regions. Mandarin is the official language of China. There are different dialects of Mandarin and it does vary from the north of the country to the south. Cantonese is a dialect spoken in Southern China in Hong Kong and Guangzhou (Canton) and throughout South East Asia. The Cantonese dialect is very different to Mandarin and they can sound like completely different languages, except that all dialects are pronounced from the same writing or characters.

Despite differences in the pronunciation of the Six Healing Sounds and variations in the movements of the various styles, they all share similar benefits.

Understanding the principles of the Chinese healing arts

When we start our journey into the Chinese healing arts there are many new ideas and concepts to understand. They are different to the exercises that many of us have been taught when we were younger or that are promoted through gyms and other sporting activities. They are even quite different to yoga which is a very popular mind and body exercise. The key to the practice is relaxation and tranquillity; to be able to move the body without too much physical or mental tension. It does take practice; a lot of practice.

It's important to grasp the basic theory and philosophy of the Chinese healing arts. Otherwise without this understanding, these ancient energy cultivation practices can become a slow motion dance or gentle exercises. To understand the theory is important, but the practice is more important. It's only through constant practice over many years that the concepts and theory become intertwined with our thought processes and it becomes natural. When this happens, the true benefits of the Chinese healing arts can be realised

The Chinese have a term for this - 'Gong Fu' (Kung Fu). 'Gong' means 'work, skill or cultivation' and 'Fu' means 'time'. Together these two words translate to 'taking the time to cultivate a skill'. Sometimes the longer it takes, the better the result will be.

Wu Ji 無 極 and Tai Ji 太 極 According to Chinese philosophy, before heaven or before creation was the state of Wu Ji. It is also known as prenatal in TCM literature. The primordial universe was in a state of nothingness, emptiness or the void, before creation as we know it; before the big bang. After the big bang came the after heaven or postnatal state of the universe; this is what the Chinese call 'Tai Ji', also popularly written as 'Tai Chi'. Something came from nothing as the classics say, the two opposing forces of Yin and Yang created the after heaven universe. This can be seen in the Tai Ji symbol which comprises of two opposing forces that balance or complement each other. Without one the other would not exist. Yang energy is expressed in qualities such as up, external, male, hot and bright. Yin energy resides in the opposing characteristics such as down, internal, female, cold and dark.

Wu Ji Symbol   Tai Ji Symbol

"Returning to the root is the direction of the subtle path.
Gentleness is the application of the subtle path.
Thus, the subtle path lasts.
All things under Heaven are born from something.
Something is born from nothing."
Lao Tzu, Dao De Jing, Chapter 40

Dao 道 or Tao translates to 'the way' or 'path'. It's not a religion but a way of connecting and harmonising with nature. Its origins are in ancient Chinese culture dating back over 5000 years. Lao Tzu, a historical figure from 500 BC, was the first great master to write about his understanding of the nature of the Dao. His book, the Dao De Jing, now forms the basis of most Daoist thought. Some of the other healing arts originating from Daoist tradition include acupuncture, Chinese herbal medicine, Qigong, Taijiquan, Feng Shui and Chinese therapeutic massage.

The Three Treasures is one of the foundation principles of Daoism and TCM. It's a way of understanding how we as human beings grow internally and connect with our environment and the universe. Unfortunately if our internal energy system is not functioning correctly this natural process will suffer and we will not fully experience the beauty of life as we should.

Jing 精 or Essence refers to all refined, subtle, and nutritious substances and is the material basis of the human body. We receive Jing in two ways: from what we are born with (prenatal), from our family heritage- a bit like energetic DNA, and we also receive essence from the fresh food, water and air that nourishes our body in the present world (postnatal). It is important to protect the Jing that has been given to us. Illness, stress and an unhealthy lifestyle will waste this precious energy.

Qi 氣 or Energy can be translated as 'natural energy', 'life force' or 'energy flow' and refers to the refined subtle essences. According to TCM, Qi controls the functional activities of the organs in the body. The Qi inherent in the prenatal state is called 'original' or 'Yuan' Qi and the Qi obtained from breathing and diet is called 'acquired' Qi. There are many different types of Qi, depending on distribution, locations and its function. There are three main aspects of Qi: 'Heaven Qi' is the Yang energy that we absorb from the universe, 'Earth Qi' is the Yin energy that we receive from this world and 'Human Qi' is the interrelationship between the energies of heaven and earth, the harmony between Yang and Yin.

Shen 神 or Spirit is the governor of life activities according to TCM theory. Shen represents the active nature of our being, including our presence, consciousness, vitality, mental functions and spiritual activities. Through the Shen we are able to project ourselves and connect with the energies of the universe and the divine. The prenatal Shen refers to the light from our original nature before birth and the postnatal Shen is sometimes called the 'acquired' or 'mind of desires' spirit.

Cultivating the Three Treasures - Essence, Energy and Spirit

The Yellow Emperor's Internal Classic says: 'The original substance of life is called Jing (Essence); the combined Yin and Yang essence is called spirit (Shen).' These internal cultivation practices are divided into four stages of cultivation: refining Jing (Essence) and converting it into Qi (Energy), refining Qi to nourish the spirit (Shen), refining Shen to return to nothingness and refining nothingness to integrate into Dao. The stage of refining essence to convert it into Qi is also termed the 'Small Heavenly Orbit Circulation'.

Dan Tian 丹田 translates to 'the cauldron where elixir is refined'. There are three Dan Tians or energy centres in the body according to Daoist and TCM understanding. They are like a storehouse or reservoir where the cultivated internal energy is stored for later use. The lower Dan Tian is situated just below the navel and is the foundation for standing, breathing and body awareness; it is where essence or Jing is refined into Qi. The middle Tan Tian is at the level of the heart and is associated with respiration and the health of the internal organs; this is also where the spirit or Shen resides and is where Qi is refined into Shen. The upper Dan Tian is between the eyebrows and is where Shen is refined into nothingness.

Traditional Chinese Medicine

An important principle underlying TCM is the understanding of the balance and harmony between human beings and our environment. Daoism and TCM view the human being as a micro (internal) representation of our macro (external) environment. It is based on the concept that the human body is a small universe with a set of complete and sophisticated interconnected systems, and that those systems usually work in balance and with the forces of nature to maintain the healthy function of the human body. TCM seeks to heal the root causes of dysfunction or disease and has been practised for over 5000 years, making it one of the oldest and most widely used systems of medicine in the world.

In this ancient vision of the body, the internal organs function differently from the way they are understood to function in Western medicine. Unlike the Western medical model which divides the physical body into anatomical structures, the Chinese model is more concerned with function. Thus, the TCM heart is not a specific piece of flesh, but an aspect of function related to consciousness, mental vitality and unclouded thinking.

Each solid organ (Yin) has a corresponding flowing organ (Yang). TCM understands that everything is composed of two complementary energies; one energy is Yin and the other is Yang. They are never separate; one cannot exist without the other. This relationship is reflected in the black and white Yin/Yang symbol. No matter how you try to divide this circle in half, each section will always contain both energies.

The organs also correspond to the Five Elements, relating to different seasons, directions, colours and emotions. The belief that the human body is a microcosm of the universal macrocosm means that humans must follow the laws of the universe to achieve harmony and total health. The Yin/Yang and Five Element theories are observations and descriptions of universal law, not concepts created by man. These essential theories form the basis of TCM and are used today to understand, diagnose and treat health problems. The network of relationships is complex and scholars study and meditate for many years to fully understand these connections between the internal and the external world.

Six Healing Sounds and The Five Elements

	木	火	土	金	水
	Wood	Fire	Earth	Metal	Water
Yin Organ	Liver	Heart	Spleen	Lungs	Kidney
Yang Organ	Gall bladder	Small Intestine	Stomach	Large Intestine	Bladder
Season	Spring	Summer	Late summer	Autumn	Winter
Color	Green	Red	Yellow	White	Deep Blue/ Black
Emotion	Anger	Joy/ Excitement	Worry	Grief	Fear
Virtues	kindness and compassion	love and peace	honesty and trust	strength and righteousness	wisdom and perception
Direction	East	South	Center	West	North
Healing Sound	Xu	Ke	Hu	Si	Chui
Pronounced	Shooo	Herrr	Huuuu	Sssir	Treeee

* The **Triple Heater**, Healing Sound Xi pronounced Sheeee

Meridians

While Western medicine recognises only three circulatory networks in the human body: the nervous system, the lymphatic system and the blood vessels, TCM includes a fourth system: the energy network of meridians. Meridians are pathways or channels which transport Qi throughout the whole body, ensuring the tissues and organs are supplied with fluids and nutrients. They are all interconnected and form a network connecting the internal organs to external parts of the body.

Meridian lines or energy channels cannot be seen or felt like other systems in the body, such as the circulatory or nervous system. When a person is in good (balanced) health, their meridian lines will be open and clear of blockages; Qi can then flow smoothly.

These meridian lines can be associated with the functioning of the body's internal organs. The health of an organ is affected by the corresponding meridian and has a direct impact on the strength and energy of the meridian. If these organs function abnormally, the energy will stagnate in the meridians and cause illness. To return to good health the blockage must be released and the flow of energy normalised.

The Twelve Organ Meridians or Energy Channels

No 1. Lung Meridian 肺经 (Yin) Nurturing. The main purpose of the lungs is respiration. According to TCM, the lungs are in charge of the Qi of the whole body.

No 2. Large Intestine Meridian 大肠经 (Yang) Dispersing. The large intestine's function is to pass and eliminate waste.

No 3. Spleen Meridian 脾经 (Yin) Nurturing. The spleen aids the digestive system and in TCM the essence received from food and water is distributed to all parts of the body.

No 4. Stomach Meridian 胃经 (Yang) Dispersing. The stomach also aids in absorption and digestion. The stomach likes to be moist, allowing the Qi to descend.

No 5. Liver Meridian 肝经 (Yin) Nurturing. The liver helps regulate and smooth the flow of blood and Qi. It promotes digestion and absorption as well as keeping Qi and blood moving normally.

No 6. Gall Bladder Meridian 胆经 (Yang) Dispersing. The gall bladder receives the bile that is made and secreted by the liver.

No 7. Kidney Meridian 肾经 **(Yin) Nurturing.** In TCM, the kidneys store the essence that is received from food and air and is released when the other organs require it. They are like the 'batteries' of the body.

No 8. Bladder Meridian 膀胱经 **(Yang) Dispersing.** After the kidneys have cleansed the fluids in the body, the clean fluids are retained and the waste is stored and excreted by the bladder.

No 9. Heart Meridian 心经 **(Yin) Nurturing.** The heart is the 'Emperor of the Body' according to ancient TCM texts. It helps control the function of the whole body.

No 10. Small Intestine Meridian 小肠经 (Yang) Dispersing. The small intestine receives, transforms and absorbs the solids and fluids, helping to separate the waste from any useful parts.

No 11. Pericardium Meridian 心包经 **(Yin) Nurturing.** The pericardium also relates to the functions of the heart.

No 12. Triple Heater (San Jiao) Meridian 三焦经 **(Yang) Dispersing.** The triple heater is a passage in which solids and fluids are heated and pass through the body.

The Meridian Cycle

Meridians are classified as Yin or Yang depending on which way they flow on the surface of the body. Yang energy flows from the sun, and Yang meridians run from the fingers to the face or from the face to the feet. Yin energy flows from the earth, and Yin meridians run from the feet to the torso and from the torso along the inside of the arms to the fingertips. Since the meridian flow is continuous and unbroken, the energy flows in one direction and from one meridian to another in a well determined order. Since there is no beginning or end to this flow, the order can be represented as a wheel. The flow around the wheel follows the meridian lines on the body in this order:

- From torso to fingertip (along inside of arm- Yin)
- From fingertip to face (along outside/back of arm- Yang)
- From face to feet (along outside of leg- Yang)
- From feet to torso (along inside of the leg- Yin)

Chapter 3
The Art of Practice

Six Healing Sounds
Nurturing Life Qigong

The Art of Practice

To get the most out of your practice there are a few basic principles and guidelines, as well as precautions that you should be aware of. These principles are important for gaining a deeper understanding and experiencing the full benefits of this ancient healing art. Proper practice ensures positive results and eliminates potential negative effects.

Relaxation and tranquillity are the fundamental requirements and methods for Qigong practice. From the external to the internal, we first start by relaxing the physical body as this helps relieve respiratory and mental tension. Tranquillity means allowing the mind to be calm and find inner peace; the practice of tranquillity in Qigong requires quiet external surroundings and a peaceful internal world. Internal tranquillity, with your mind relaxed and focused, is more important than external silence. Relaxing can induce tranquillity while tranquillity helps relaxing. Complete relaxation is possible only when complete tranquillity is present.

Correct practice helps induce the effect of relaxation and tranquillity, whereas incorrect postures may inhibit one's ability to realise this state of relaxation and tranquillity. Correct postures and movements take time to master and are dependent on the individual's specific physiological and psychological characteristics at their stage of practice. The difficulty and intensity of practice should be adjusted according to the person, the time, the place and their attained state, in order to produce the desired mental and physical relaxation. Otherwise, improper practice may produce only stress and fatigue.

Making it a pleasurable experience as you progress from beginner to advanced level, is a fundamental principle in learning Qigong. We should practise persistently over a long period of time; Qigong practice is a process of constant accumulation. As long as one perseveres with the practice, the effects will be obtained gradually and naturally. Some students show significant improvements within a short period of time, whereas some practitioners do not display any distinctive changes for a long time, and some may start with positive effects which soon diminish. Whatever the effects, it is important to have a correct and positive attitude. Being confident about oneself and persistent in practice is important. Qigong is a practical method, and long-term practice is the only way to experience real benefits. It's common to experience different sensations when practising Qigong. Feeling warmth and a tingling sensation in different parts of the body is common, as well as the rising of emotions and some people even report seeing different colours and visions. Try not to place too much attention on sensations as it can deplete your Qi experience. It's better to go to the level of no sensation and return to nothingness.

Meditation and processing the Qi

Our thinking mind uses the most energy of our body; when the mind is calm and relaxed it can increase our energy, whereas when the mind is very active it can deplete our energy. After practising the dynamic moving sections of the Six Healing Sounds, we practise the static or stillness section. This part of our practice is very important; when the body comes to a complete stop, the Qi keeps moving and through the tranquillity of the mind, the Qi will come into order. It's what we call the 'processing' stage; it's important to keep your thinking mind out of the way and to allow the Qi to do its work. The movements clear the meridian system, dispel stale Qi and absorb good Qi, helping foster Yang with tranquillity breeding Yin. To balance Yin and Yang we need a good balance between dynamic and static; too much movement or stillness by itself can unbalance Yin and Yang.

Where and when to practise?

Exercising in the early morning and late afternoon when the sun rises and sets is a very powerful time, as there is a natural transition between the dark coolness of night (Yin) and the bright warmth of day (Yang). The setting of the sun and transition between Yang and Yin is also a time when nature has a great influence on your body. It's important not to look directly into the sun in the early morning or late afternoon, as this can cause damage to your eyes. You might notice that birds are very active at this time of day, as they are in the morning.

Qigong can be practised anywhere, but some places are better than others. You should be undisturbed during Qigong practice to help maintain concentration in the mind. The best places are in nature in the open air where the Heaven Qi (Yang) and Earth Qi (Yin) are most abundant. Practise in the mountains or beside a waterfall or the ocean; near water is excellent because moving water generates a lot of Qi.

If you are practising indoors, try to find a quiet and peaceful space away from draughts with natural light and fresh air. Avoid excessive noise, TV sets and computers and turn off your mobile phone or set it to silent.

The proximity of some plants should also be avoided. The Oleander plant for example, is known to be poisonous and has a very tense Qi. As you practise you will learn which plants feel relaxing and harmonious. Lovely flowers and large old trees are ideal.

As a rule, you should not exercise on a full or empty stomach. Instead of eating breakfast, consume liquids as they stimulate stomach-intestine movement which acts as an internal massage. Warm or room temperature water is the best with a slice of lemon, but not cold water from the fridge, as this interferes with Qi circulation.

Qigong exercise in the evenings is a way of freeing your mind and body from the burdens of a busy day; a way of processing the events of the day and letting things go, physically and emotionally. Students often comment on how they get their best night's sleep after attending class. You are able to sleep more quietly and recover more fully because the body begins its recovery during Qigong and this continues during sleep.

We are all a bit different, so I wouldn't advise anyone practising just before going to sleep as it stimulates your energy and may disrupt your sleep. But a few students have told me that when they haven't been able to sleep, they would get up and practise Qigong to calm their mind and body, then have a restful sleep afterwards.

Eating and drinking

For Qigong exercise you need a clear head. Beverages such as alcohol, tea and coffee affect concentration and your body's functions. If you are not calm and relaxed you will not feel the full benefits from Qigong exercise. It's best to avoid drinking cold fluids during or immediately after practice as this interferes with Qi circulation.

You should not exercise on either an empty stomach or after a full meal. Being distracted by hunger will not help your mental focus, so if you are hungry have something light to eat or something to drink. A full stomach interferes with Qi circulation. The Qi is diverted into the digestive system, as stomach juices increase and stomach-intestinal movements occur, leaving very little Qi to circulate elsewhere.

When not to exercise

When we exercise we absorb the good influences from nature and the macrocosm. Similarly, we assimilate the influences from turbulent weather conditions. Therefore, it is not good to practise Qigong during bad weather, heavy fog, extreme heat, before or during a thunderstorm, on excessively windy days, or during lunar or solar eclipses. Exercise can begin again when nature is balanced.

Menstruation and pregnancy

Qigong is good to practise during menstruation and pregnancy as it will improve the circulation of Qi, blood and other bodily fluids.

Women who are menstruating should pay attention to the effects of Qigong exercise. If the exercise produces a negative effect, stop immediately and continue at a later time.

Special care is also required during pregnancy. Each woman's pregnancy is different and it is recommended that the expectant mother consult her primary care provider as well as a qualified and experienced Qigong teacher.

What to wear?

There are no rules regarding clothing but since relaxation is important in Qigong, try to wear loose comfortable clothing, ideally made of natural fibres such as cotton or silk. If you are limited in what you can wear, for example if you are at work, loosen your collar and tie, your belt or waistband and remove uncomfortable or high-heeled shoes. It's important that you wear flat-soled shoes and even bare feet are OK. I always wear soft sports shoes as I damaged my feet and ankles a long time ago and I find wearing shoes gives me a bit more support. It's a personal preference and there are many light soft shoes available that are suitable.

Whatever clothing you choose to wear, it should not be tight around the waist because the Qi needs to flow easily. Preferably, remove watches and bracelets as they restrict the flow of Qi through the wrist.

If it is chilly, dress appropriately. Feeling cold during a Qigong session can decrease the effectiveness of the exercises, particularly if your hands, stomach or back are cold; chilling your kidneys severely restricts your Qi circulation. I often start my practice on colder mornings with gloves, hat and a warm jacket; you can always take them off when you heat up.

How long to practise?

The benefits that are gained from Qigong are proportional to the amount of practice undertaken. It is only when the body's carriage is regulated according to Qigong principles that the Qi will flow easily and the benefits of Qigong realised. If you can achieve thirty minutes twice a day, you will notice a marked increase in vitality and peace within a few weeks. If you have major health issues and can manage a couple of hours per day, you will soon see a radical improvement in your health and wellbeing. Regardless of your state of health when you begin, any amount of regular practice will improve how you feel.

How long does the effect of Qigong exercise last?

Qigong works because the Qi is brought into order and the mind, body and spirit are in harmony. This harmony can be disturbed by arguing, getting excited or annoyed, engaging in strenuous physical activity, eating excessively and even going to the toilet. If possible, use the toilet beforehand rather than after Qigong exercise because urination and defecation bring the Qi into definite motion.

I often tell my students after a Qigong class that if they have driven a car there not to play the radio when they leave, as all your senses have been enhanced and the body functions are in harmony. You may get good ideas, solve some problems or if you are with friends you may have amazing conversations. Look at the beauty of the sky, trees and the divine in all living things; I love to look at clouds. It's a creative time, so use it and the Qi will be with you longer. The more you cultivate your Qi the more in harmony with the universe you will be, improving all aspects of your life.

Chapter 4
Qigong Preparation – Warm-up

Six Healing Sounds
Nurturing Life Qigong

Qigong Preparation – Warm-up

It's important to relax the mind as well as relax the body, because one cannot thoroughly relax the body without relaxing the mind. We should be uninterrupted and the movements slow, soft and smooth.

Qigong is a cultivation exercise which benefits the physical body, the energetic or Qi body as well as the mind. It allows us to rebalance our mind, body and breath and with regular practice it enables us to create a healthy lifestyle and to help identify our true spiritual nature.

It is important to create the right conditions before, during and after practice to get the best results. According to the ancient Daoist way of understanding our relationship and connection with the universe, we allow our internal landscape to harmonise with the external landscape.

It is important to prepare the mind, body and breath before we start to practise. Qigong practices abide by the basic principles of the three 'adjustments' or three 'tunings'. These are a way of calming the mental activity of the brain and turning on and tuning the mind, to tune into the breath and the body.

*   **Tuning the Body**
*   **Tuning the Breath**
*   **Tuning the Mind**

Qigong should never be practised when you are feeling physically cold, energetically cold or emotionally cold. The Qi will not flow very well and can even have an adverse effect. Good preparation is equally as important as a good practice and a good close.

The warm-up is not only a way of preparing the mind and body for the Qigong movements that follow, it is also very good exercise. Physically, when we loosen and rotate the joints, we exercise the ligaments and tendons as well as the membranes which secrete synovial fluid to lubricate the joints. This can improve many arthritic conditions. Energetically, we clear stagnant energy (Qi) that can accumulate around the joints. The stretching movements also help stimulate the meridian system as well as strengthen the muscular system. According to TCM, Qi draws the blood through the body. So when we stimulate the Qi circulation we also stimulate blood circulation.

Generally, when we have finished the warm-up, we feel warm, tingling and have turned on and tuned into the body, breath and mind.

Preparing the mind

During the preparation and warm-up we first concentrate on the mind and allow the excess Yang energy or activity of the brain to descend down. When we have too much activity in this area it can be very hard to concentrate. We keep our mind in the present moment by initially concentrating on the flow of the breath. In time the breath will become smooth and even and this will allow your mind to rest.

When we are in this relaxed state we can use our intention and direct our awareness, like the light of a torch, on each part of the body as we are exercising it, from head to toe. Through this active meditation we consciously awaken the body by feeling and seeing what we are doing.

Preparing the posture and breath

Keep the body upright with the head and spine naturally in alignment; allow the muscles and flesh to relax around the skeleton. The movements of Qigong help clear the energy blockages in our body. With time and practice the movements will become natural and effortless.

There are a number of different breathing patterns for different styles of Qigong. For the styles presented here, we will breathe in and out through the nose to the abdominal area, slowly, deeply and naturally. When we breathe in, the abdomen gently expands and when we breathe out, it gently contracts. This is known as natural breathing. In time, the breath will naturally coordinate with the movements, helping the mind to focus and allowing a fusion between mind, body and breath.

Basic stance

Stand with your feet parallel, shoulder width apart, as if standing on train tracks, with the knees slightly off lock. Let your weight sink into your legs, feet and into the ground. Keep the coccyx or tail bone slightly tucked in, chest relaxed, and the back straight. Hold your arms away from the body. Fingers are open and relaxed and pointing to the earth; palms are facing the body.

With the chin slightly tucked in, the top of the head (Bai Hui point) reaches towards the sky as if a silken cord attached to it is lifting the whole body. Lift the Hui Yin and gently squeeze the pelvic floor. Relax your eyes and face and look out into the distance. Keep your jaw relaxed and place the tip of your tongue on the top palate of your mouth, just behind the front teeth. Breathe in and out through the nose. When breathing in, let the abdomen push out slightly and as the breath goes out, let the abdomen come in. Just relax, letting the whole body breathe.

With the eyes closed, allow the breath to become smooth and even and let your mind rest. After a few breaths, concentrate on the out breath and relax from the top of the head to the soles of the feet. Just relax down through the body on the out breath.

After a few more breaths, let the knees and hips sink a bit closer to the ground and feel the pressure go into the feet. Like a tree, follow the roots from the soles of your feet deeply into the ground. As you let the breath out, relax down through the body into the ground, letting the stress and tension of the body dissolve into the earth.

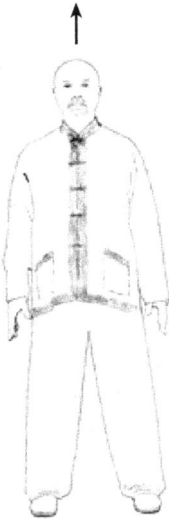

After another few breaths, with your awareness, push up the spine one vertebra at a time, checking that the chin tucks in a bit and let the head pull away from the body. We seem to stand taller as the top of the head reaches up and touches the sky. Stay in this posture for a few breaths, feeling the peace. With your eyes gradually opening, look out into the distance, but not looking.

The Warm-Up Movements

Arm and chest stretch

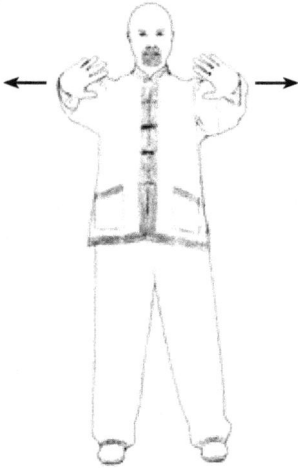 

1a   1a (side view)

 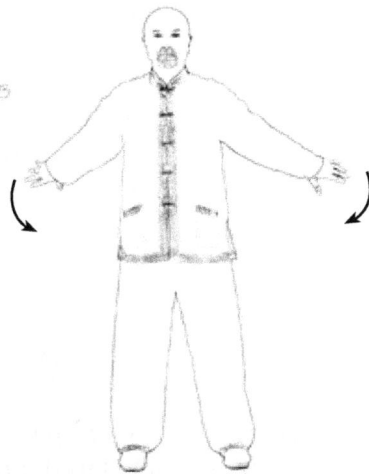

1b   1c

1a-c Raise both arms up in front of the body to about shoulder height. Turn your palms out and push to the sides, feeling your chest and rib cage open. Push back and stretch back as far as comfortable.

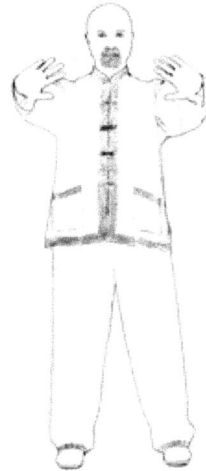

1e (side view)   **1e**   **1f**

1g

1d-g Turn your palms up, bend the elbows and bring the hands to the front of the body, brushing by the waist. Repeat four times, similar to swimming breaststroke.

1h   **1i (side view)**   **1j**

1h-j   Then repeat four times in the opposite direction. With palms up, hands brush by your waist and stretch behind; slowly rotate palms and bring arms in front of the body.

This movement exercises the chest, shoulders, elbows and wrists.

Body roll

2a-b Let your arms slowly descend to your sides. Slowly roll one shoulder and then the other, like swimming backstroke. With your awareness, feel the motion massage your shoulders, chest, abdomen, and your back over the kidney area.

2a   2b

2c-d After about eight rotations, stop and come back the other way, rotating forward, feeling the internal massage.

2c   2d

Hip rotations

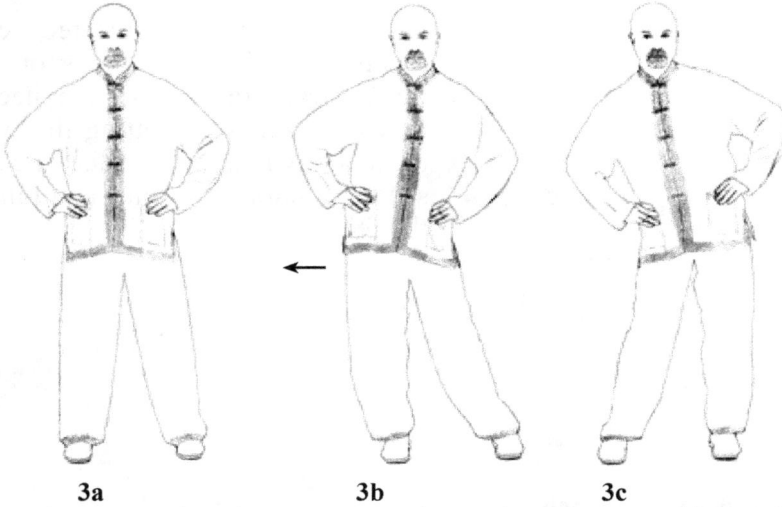

3a   3b   3c

3a-c   Place your hands on your waist and start to move your hips from side to side. Relax and feel the movement of the hips.

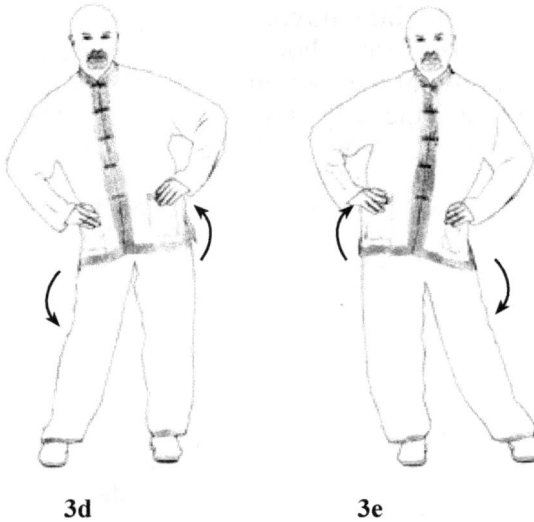

3d   3e

3d-e   After about three movements to each side, start to move the hips in a circle, gradually increasing your range of movement. Follow the spiraling movement up the spine to the top of your head. Feel and see the movement of the hips. After about six rotations, stop and come back the other way.

Walking and massaging the feet

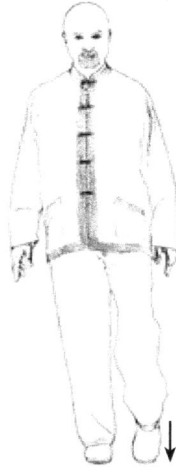

4a-b Stand with your feet closer together, walking on the spot. Push firmly from the toe to the heel six times to each side, letting the weight of the body massage the feet. Feel and see the tendons, muscles and joints of the feet.

4a (side view)　　　**4b**

4c-d Turn and twist while moving your knee across the body, massaging the inside of the foot on the floor towards the big toe. Repeat about six times to each side.

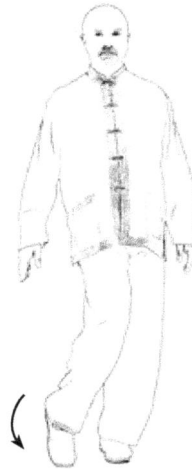
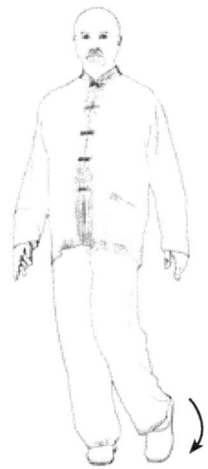

4c　　　**4d**

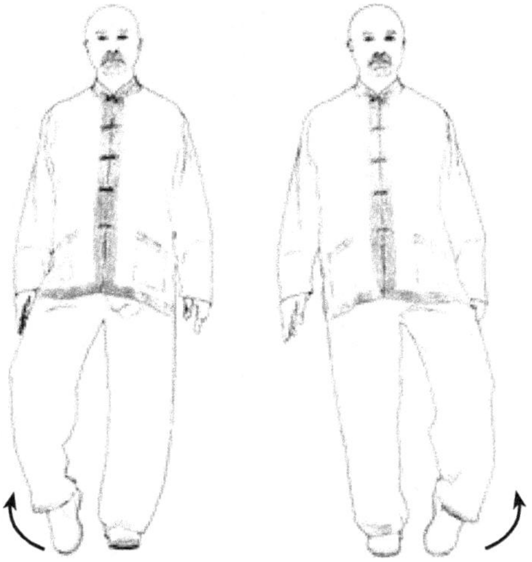

4e-f Stop and push to the outside of the foot, massaging towards the small toe, six to each side. Relax, feel and see the movement of the foot.

4e

4f

Shaking the legs

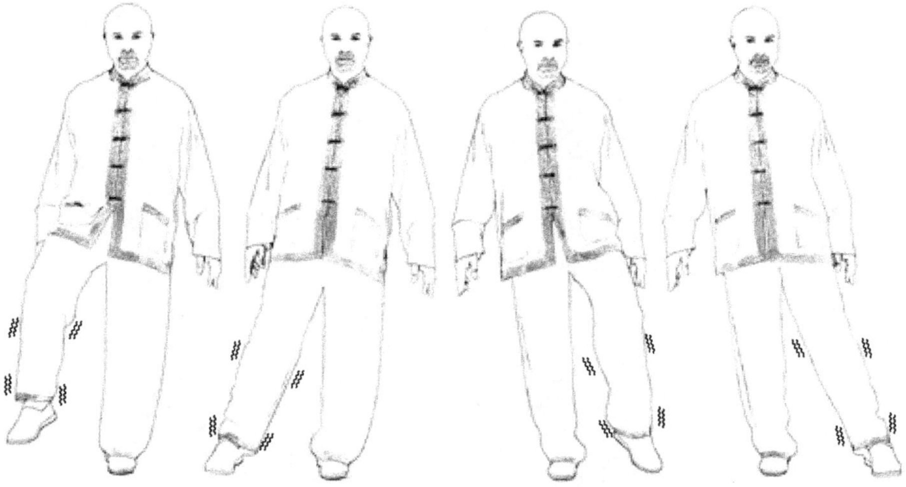

5a

5b

5c

5d

5a-d Shake your legs three times to each side, allowing the Qi and blood to flow.

Hand and wrist shaking

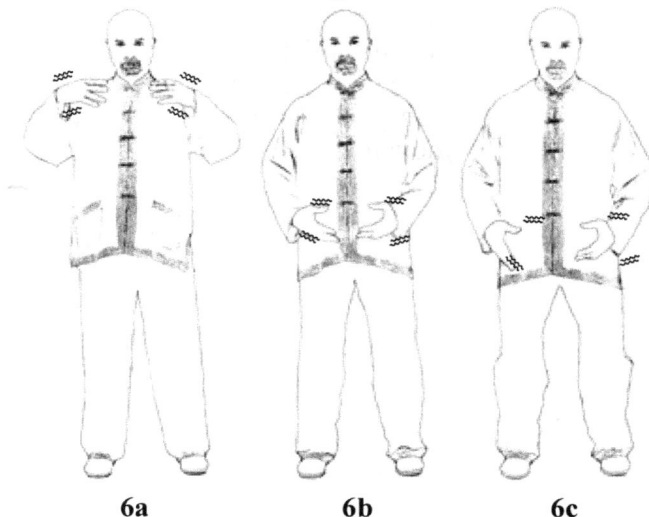

6a-c Shake your hands up and down about six times, loosening the hands.

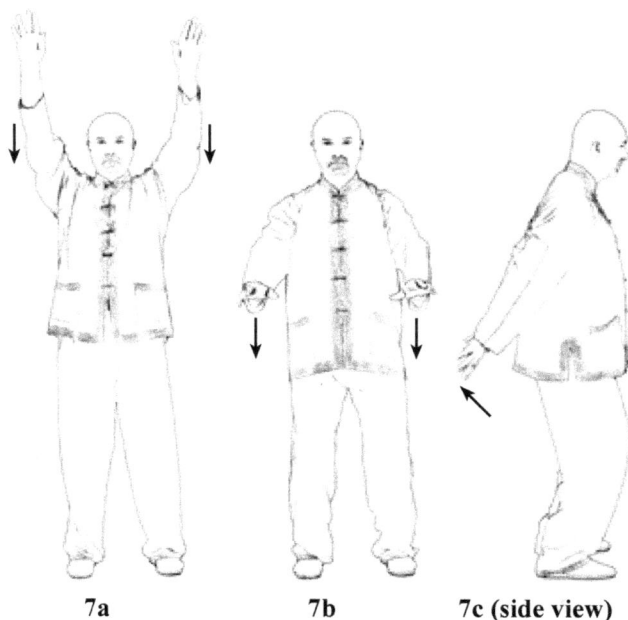

6a   6b   6c

7a   7b   7c (side view)

Body swings

7a-c With the feet parallel and arms above the head, swing the arms down, sinking the knees at the same time. Let the whole body swing; keep the back straight and head upright.

With your awareness, relax the shoulders and hips, elbows and knees, wrists and ankles, hands and feet. Do this for about twelve swings. This helps strengthen the whole body and is good for blood circulation.

Swinging arms

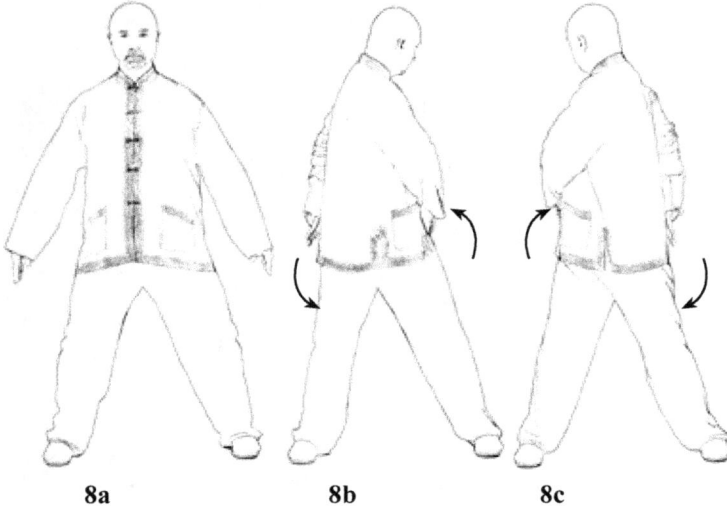

8a   8b   8c

8a-c Step out to a wider horse-riding stance. With the legs grounded firmly and the arms relaxed, let your arms swing out while turning from the waist. Let the arms slap across the body, massaging around the waist and hips.

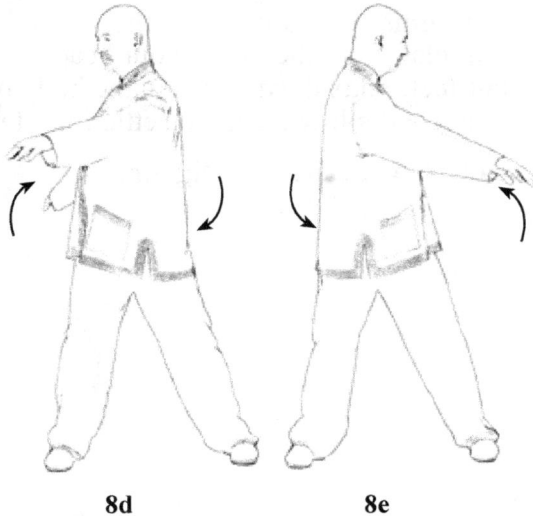

8d   8e

8d-e Let your arms swing higher, massaging around the kidneys and finally, higher again as one swinging arm taps the shoulder while the other taps the kidneys. Do this twelve times. This helps loosen and strengthen the back and massage the internal organs.

Closing Qi

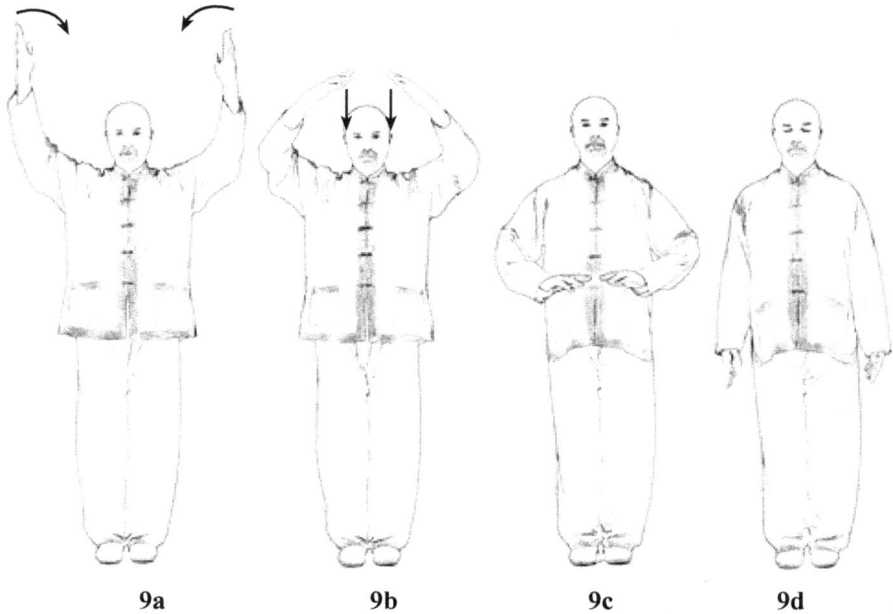

9a   9b   9c   9d

9a-d   Stand with your feet together; raise your hands up above your head guiding the Qi down the body from the top of the head to the soles of your feet. Your arms rest naturally at the side of your body. With your eyes closed, relax from the top of your head down to your hands and down to your feet; relax down through the body on the out breath. Stay in this position and allow the Qi to settle for a few minutes.

We are now ready to practise our Qigong.

Chapter 5
The Six Healing Sounds

Six Healing Sounds
Nurturing Life Qigong

The Six Healing Sounds

Liu Zi Jue 六字訣

The Six Healing Sounds are used to reduce disease causing factors in the six Yin meridians. Practising the healing sounds can help us recover from diseases and achieve longevity. The healing sounds clear heat in the channels and in the organs, so the organs and the body are cooled and negative emotions are released. By using the specific shape of the lips and vocalising the Six Healing Sounds, exhaling the old and inhaling the new can help regulate the Qi of the organs.

When we practise the Six Healing Sounds, it's recommended to practise six repetitions for each sound. It's important not to deviate from the instruction the ancient masters have passed down. When we start to practise, it's recommended starting with a louder sound to remove stale Qi, then gradually dropping the voice to a whisper or to no sound at all. A softer sound is more beneficial in resonating with the internal organs.

When practising the complete set of the Six Healing Sounds, we begin with a special preparation breath. The nose is related to Yang and receives energy through the in breathe from the heavens. The mouth is related to Yin and dispels stale energy and toxins from the body on the out breath to the earth.

After settling into the basic standing posture, we start by concentrating on breathing in and out through the nose for a total of six times. Then we change to breathing in through the nose and out through the mouth for a total of six times. It's important not to force the out breath, just allow the stale energy to be released through the mouth into the earth. Then we go back to doing another six breaths in and out though the nose, which stabilises our internal energy system before we start our practice.

If practising an individual or standalone section of the Six Healing Sounds, we close the Qi after each section by placing the hands on the Dan Tian. If practising the Six Healing Sounds as a continuous set of movements we close after the sixth sound by placing the hands on the Dan Tian.

After practising the complete set of Six Healing Sounds we finish with Closing and Processing the Qi see page 79.

Section No 1. Xu – Liver

嘘

The Wood Element
Relates to the Liver (Yin) and Gall Bladder (Yang)

The Wood Element corresponds to: the season of spring and windy weather, the direction of east, the colour green and the time associated with the liver is 1 am to 3 am. The emotion that stagnates in the liver is anger. Yet when anger is released, the virtue of kindness appears.

The liver helps cleanse and regulate the flow of blood in the body. According to TCM the liver's function of smoothing and regulating the flow of vital energy and blood helps the free flow of Qi throughout the whole body. It also helps the spleen, sending food essence up and the stomach sending food contents down, helping digestion become normal.

The healing sound is Xu, pronounced 'Shooo'.

Keys points for the Liver sound

1. When making the Xu sound your lips are curled as if puckering up with the tongue in a natural mid section of the mouth.
2. Grip the toes firmly, lift and squeeze the Hui Yin (pelvic floor) and open the eyes wide when making the Xu sound.

肝经 Liver Meridian

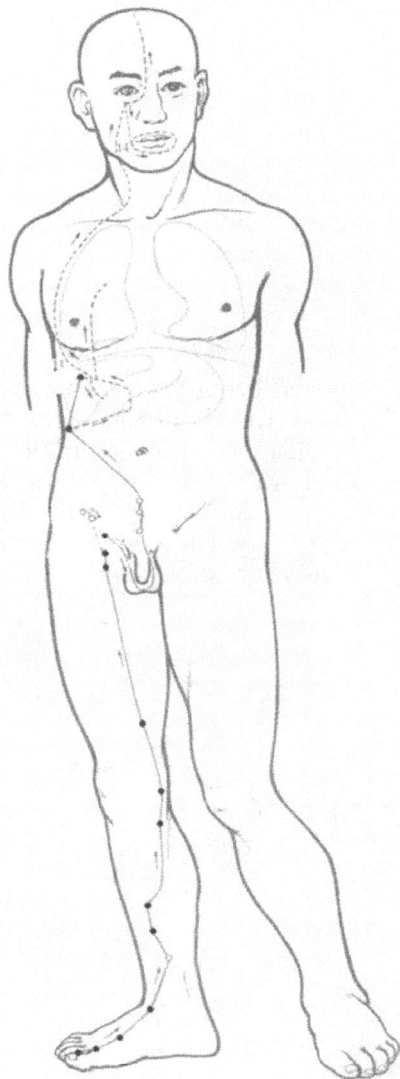

The Liver Meridian (Yin) originates at the inside of the big toe, rises up inside of the leg into the body passes through the hip, and finishes at the lower rib area.

Section No 1. Xu – Liver

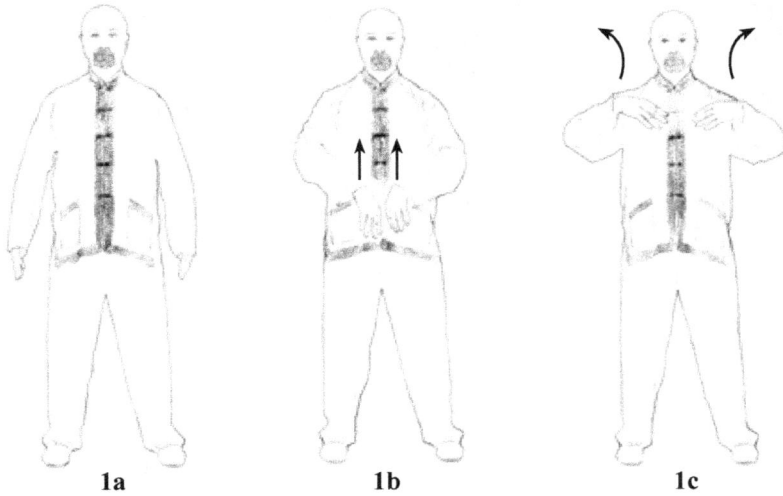

1a   1b   1c

1a-c With your eyes closed bring your awareness to the liver on the right hand side of the body for about ten seconds. Gently open your eyes, looking out to the distance, but not really looking. With your hands relaxed at the side of your body, keep your shoulders relaxed and gently bend your elbows and move your arms to the centre with the palms facing towards your body. Breathe in and raise your arms to the centre of the chest with your shoulders relaxed and your fingers pointing to the ground.

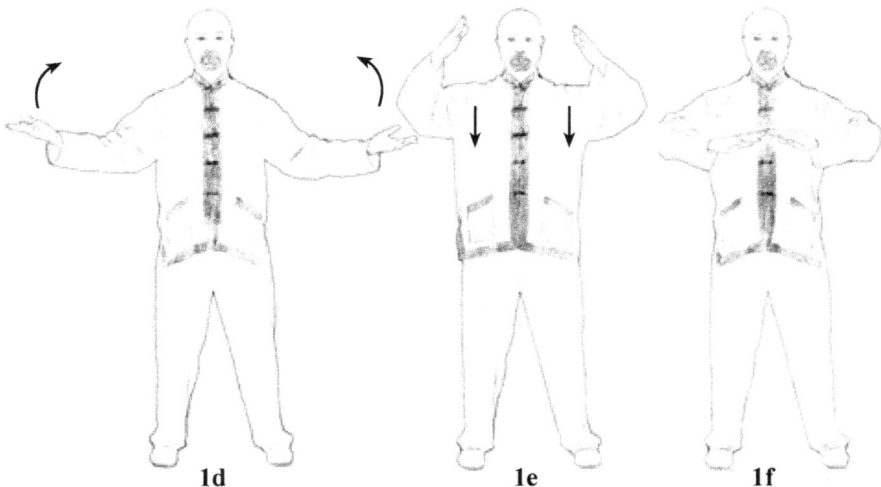

1d   1e   1f

1d-f Keeping your shoulders relaxed, open both arms in a circular movement to the side of the body, still breathing in. Your palms are facing the sky at shoulder height as if holding a large ball. Breathe out with the Xu sound, gripping your toes, lifting, squeezing the Hui Yin (pelvic floor) and opening your eyes wide.

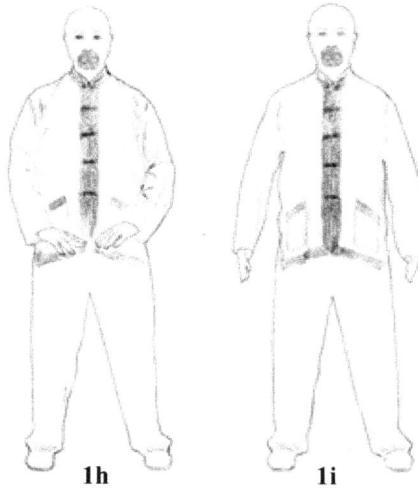

1h   **1i**

1h-i   At the same time move your arms towards the centre of the body with the palms facing towards the earth and in coordination with the Xu sound gently guide your arms and Qi down the front of the body.

Repeat for a total of six times.

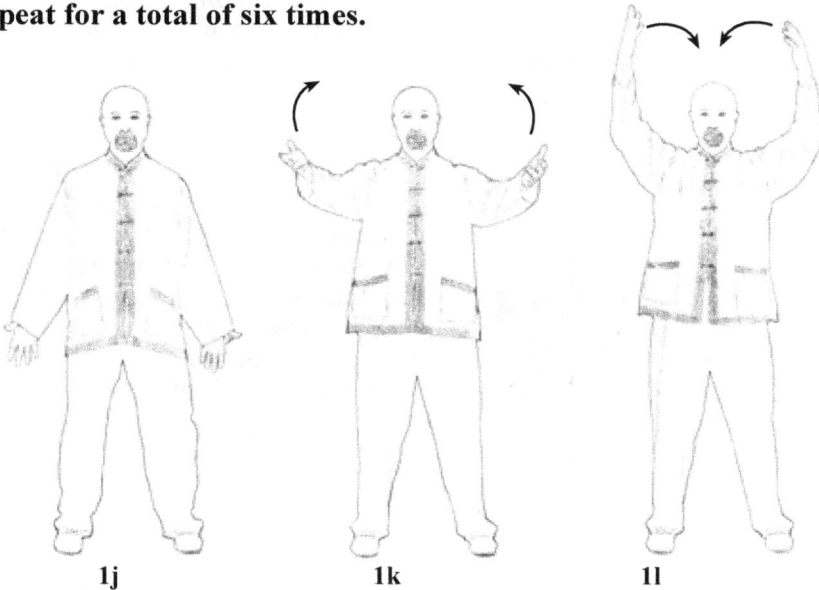

1j   **1k**   **1l**

1j-l   **Closing-** Scoop your hands out, gathering the Earth Qi (Yin), then lift up in front of body over the head while breathing in. Gather the Heaven Qi (Yang) to the top of the head (Bai Hui point), breathing out, and gently guiding the hands and Qi down in front of the body, palms facing down.

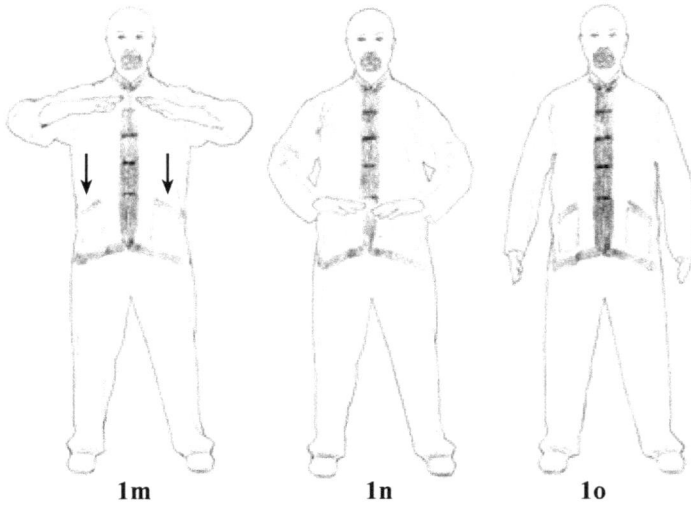

1m   1n   1o

1m-o Separate the hands as they reach the Dan Tian (navel), with fingers pointing to the ground. Allow the Heaven Qi to permeate the body both inside and out like an energy shower, cleansing and healing the whole body to the soles of the feet to the Yong Chuan (Gushing Spring point) and into the earth. Stand with your hands relaxed at the side of your body for about 30 seconds allowing the Qi to settle; relax and feel.

If practising the Six Healing Sounds as a continuous set of movements, the final closing movement, with the hands on the Dan Tian is not done until after the sixth movement. If practising individual sections only, always close with the hands on the Dan Tian.

1p

1p   Gently move your hands in front of the body. Interlock the hands with the tip of your right thumb touching the left Lao Gong (middle of palm); relax the hands and fingers. The hands make a natural Yin/Yang shape. Place your hands over the Lower Dan Tian (area beneath the navel) and close the eyes in meditation.

Section No 2. He – Heart

The Fire Element
Relates to the Heart (Yin) and Small Intestine (Yang)

The Fire Element corresponds to: the season of summer and hot weather, the direction of south, the colour red and the time associated with the heart is 11 am to 1 pm. The heart is known as the 'Emperor' of the body. When the Emperor is secure and happy, the 'kingdom' or body functions are happy. The emotions of excitement and joy can affect the functions of the heart and stop the Emperor from governing. We can create order by simply 'being'. This releases the excess emotion and the virtue of acceptance and love emerges.

The heart is the main organ of the body. Its continuous beat propels the blood to flow and circulate within the blood vessels and throughout the whole body. In TCM the heart is also the control centre; it's where the spirit or divine energy resides. When the heart or Emperor is happy, the body or kingdom will be in perfect harmony with the universe.

The healing sound is He, pronounced 'Herrr'

Keys points for the Heart sound

1. When making the He sound, the tongue is on the lower palate of the mouth just behind the teeth.
2. Keep your eyes open.

心经　Heart Meridian

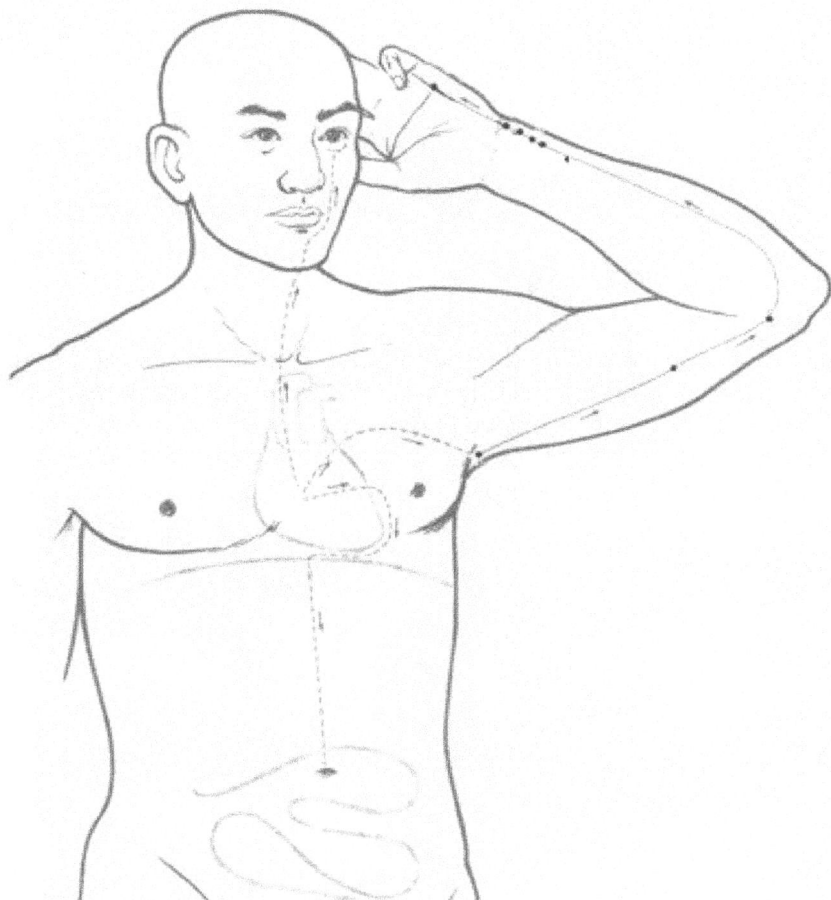

The Heart Meridian (Yin) originates at the armpit, passes through the elbow to the outside of the wrist finishing at the end of the inside of the small finger.

Section No 2. He – Heart

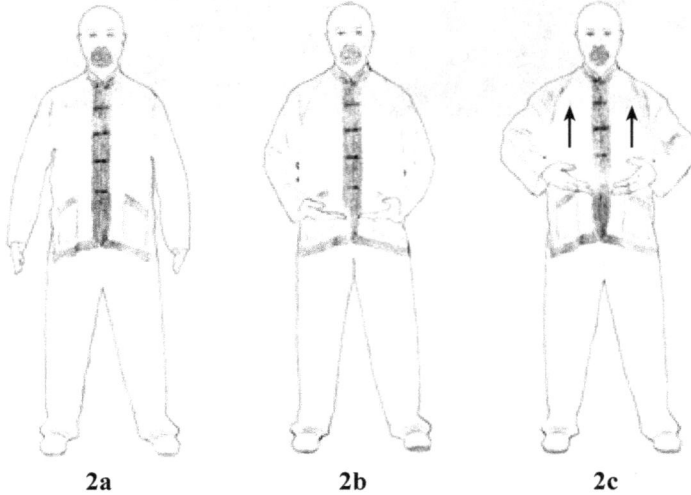

2a   2b   2c

2a-c With your eyes closed, bring your awareness to the heart for about ten seconds. Gently open your eyes, looking out to the distance, but not really looking. With your hands relaxed at the side of your body, keep your shoulders relaxed and gently scoop your hands in front of the body. Hold your palms facing up, as if holding a large ball in your arms at navel height (Dan Tian). Pause with one in and out breath.

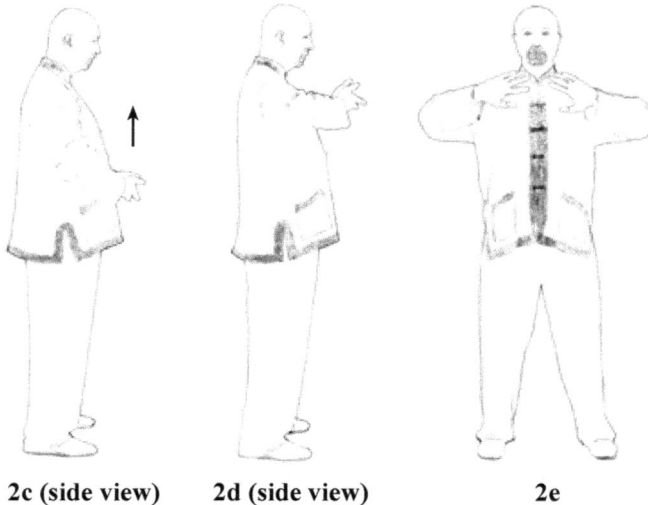

2c (side view)   2d (side view)   2e

2c-e Breathe in and slowly raise the hands to chest height. Turn the hands in and rotate towards the body with your palms facing out.

![Illustrations of figures 2f through 2i showing the He sound movements]

2f   **2g (side view)**   **2h (side view)**   **2i**

2f-i   Breathe out with the He sound and at the same time slowly move the arms away and then back towards your body with the hands making a circle. Turn the palms down to face the earth at chest height and gently guide your arms and Qi down the front of the body.

Repeat for a total of six times.
Only pause with a breath for the first movement.

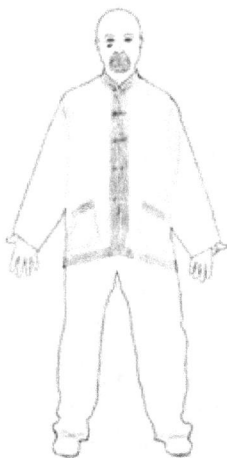

2j   **2k**   **2l**

2j-l   **Closing**- Scoop your hands out, gathering the Earth Qi (Yin), then lift up in front of the body over the head while breathing in. Gather the Heaven Qi (Yang) to the top of the head (Bai Hui point), breathing out, and gently guiding the hands and Qi down in front of the body, palms facing down.

2m   2n   2o

2m-o Separate the hands as they reach the Dan Tian (navel), with fingers pointing to the ground. Allow the Heaven Qi to permeate the body both inside and out like an energy shower, cleansing and healing the whole body to the soles of the feet to the Yong Chuan (Gushing Spring point) and into the earth. Stand with your hands relaxed at the side of your body for about 30 seconds allowing the Qi to settle; relax and feel.

If practising the Six Healing Sounds as a continuous set of movements, the final closing movement, with the hands on the Dan Tian is not done until after the sixth movement. If practising individual sections only, always close with the hands on the Dan Tian.

2p

2p   Gently move your hands in front of the body. Interlock the hands with the tip of your right thumb touching the left Lao Gong (middle of palm); relax the hands and fingers. The hands make a natural Yin/Yang shape. Place your hands over the Lower Dan Tian (area beneath the navel) and close the eyes in meditation.

Section No 3. Hu – Spleen

The Earth Element
Relates to the Spleen (Yin) and Stomach (Yang)

The Earth Element corresponds to: the late Indian summer and the climate of humidity, a central position, a golden yellow colour and the time associated with the spleen is 9 am to 11 am. The emotions of deep thinking and worry stagnate in the spleen. Yet when worry is released, the virtue of honesty emerges.

The spleen is located in the abdominal area of the body and is the main organ of the digestive system in TCM; the functions of the pancreas also relate to the spleen according to TCM. The mouth relates to the spleen; it is where food and fluids enter the body. The stomach digests the food sending the solids and fluids down and the essence of these nutrients is sent up to the spleen, the spleen transforms this essence and distributes it to the rest of the body.

The healing sound is Hu, pronounced 'Huuu'.

Keys points for the Spleen sound

1. When making the Hu sound, the tongue is in the middle of the mouth with the tip curled up.
2. Three movements to each side with the left hand going up first.
3. Keep your eyes open.

脾经　Spleen Meridian

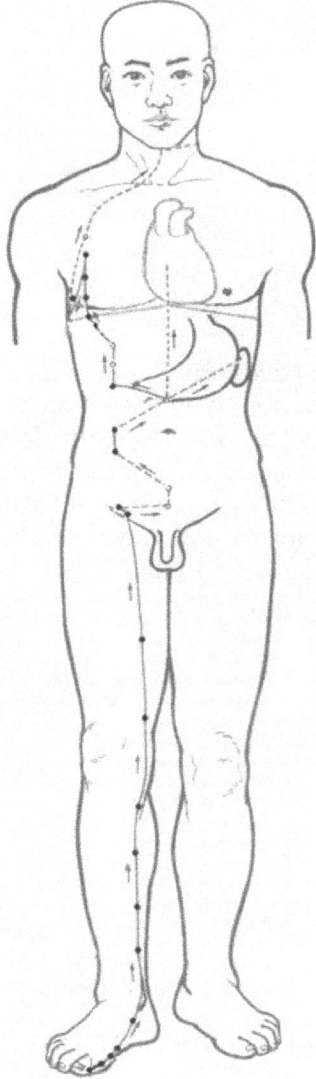

The Spleen Meridian (Yin) originates at the outside of the big toe, and rises up through the ankle, and the inside of the leg to the hip, through the abdomen to the chest and up to the oesophagus and under the tongue.

Section No 3. Hu – Spleen

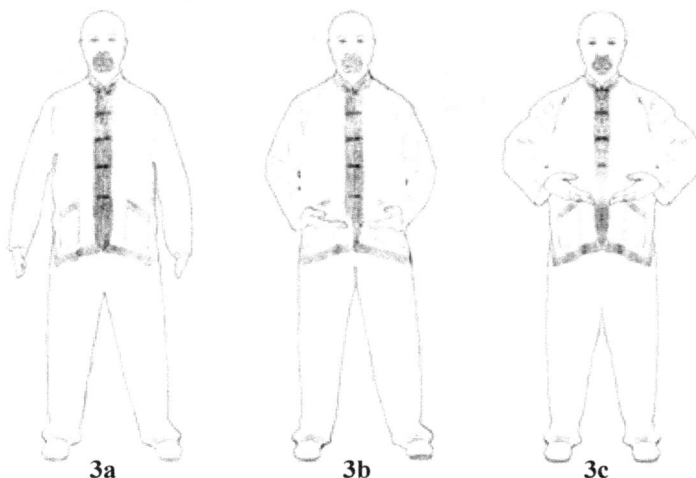

3a   3b   3c

3a-c   With your eyes closed, bring your awareness to the spleen on the left hand side of the body for about ten seconds. Gently open your eyes, looking out to the distance, but not really looking. With your hands relaxed at the side of the body, keep your shoulders relaxed and gently scoop your hands in front of the body. Hold your palms facing up, as if holding a large ball in your arms at navel height (Dan Tian). Pause with one in and out breath. Breathe in and slowly raise your arms to chest height.

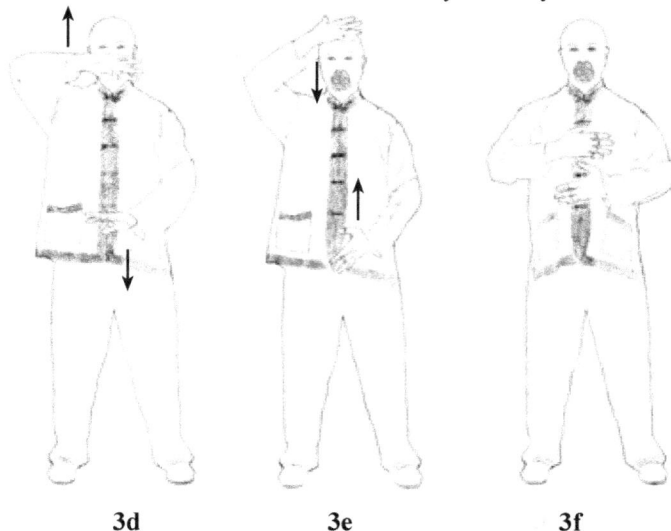

3d   3e   3f

3d-f   Slowly turn the left palm to face the sky and the right palm to face the earth. Breathe out with the Hu sound and gently separate the hands pushing up to no higher than the forehead height (Upper Dan Tian) and down no lower than the navel (Lower Dan Tian). Breathe in and slowly return arms to the middle of the chest with the top or left hand closest to your body.

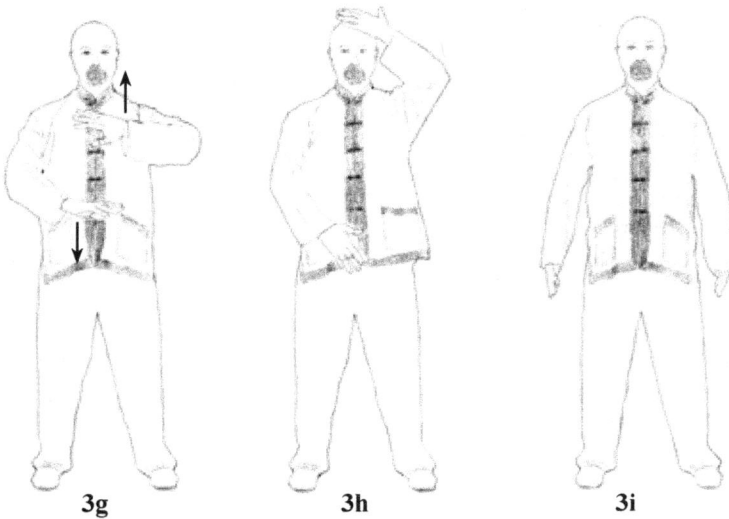

3g   3h   3i

3g-i   Slowly turn the right palm to face the sky and the left palm to face the earth. Breathe out with the Hu sound and gently separate the hands pushing up to no higher than forehead height (Upper Dan Tian) and down no lower than the navel (Lower Dan Tian). Breathe in and slowly return the arms to the middle of the chest with the top or right hand closest to your body.

Repeat three to each side for a total of six times.
Only pause with a breath for the first movement.

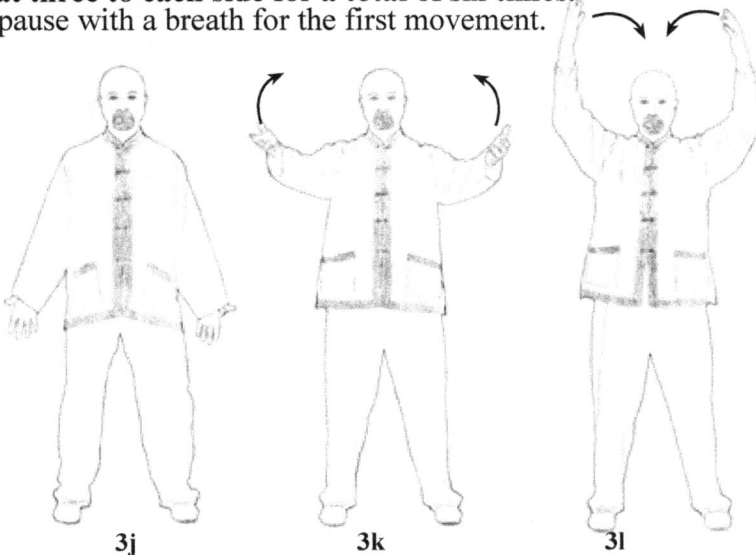

3j   3k   3l

3j-l   Closing- Scoop your hands out, gathering the Earth Qi (Yin), then up in front of the body over the head, breathing in. Gather the Heaven Qi (Yang) to the top of the head (Bai Hui point), breathing out, and gently guiding the hands and Qi down in front of the body, palms facing down.

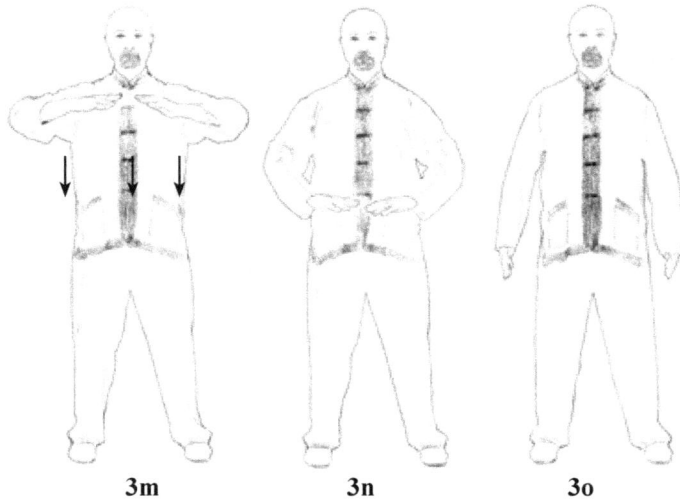

| 3m | 3n | 3o |

3m-o Separate the hands as they reach the Dan Tian (navel), with fingers pointing to the ground. Allow the Heaven Qi to permeate the body both inside and out like an energy shower, cleansing and healing the whole body to the soles of the feet to the Yong Chuan (Gushing Spring point) and into the earth. Stand with your hands relaxed at the side of your body for about 30 seconds allowing the Qi to settle; relax and feel.

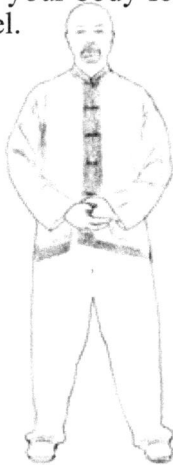

If practising the Six Healing Sounds as a continuous set of movements, the final closing movement, with the hands on the Dan Tian is not done until after the sixth movement. If practising individual sections only, always close with the hands on the Dan Tian.

3p

3p Gently move your hands in front of the body. Interlock the hands with the tip of your right thumb touching the left Lao Gong (middle of palm); relax the hands and fingers. The hands make a natural Yin/Yang shape. Place your hands over the Lower Dan Tian (area beneath the navel) and close the eyes in meditation.

Section No 4. Si – Lungs

The Metal Element
Relates to the Lung (Yin) and Large Intestine (Yang)

The Metal Element corresponds to: the season of autumn and dry weather, the direction of west, a silver/white colour and the time associated with the lungs is 3 am to 5 am. The emotion that stagnates in the lungs is sadness or grief. Yet when sadness and grief are released, the virtue of strength and righteousness emerges.

The lungs' main purpose is respiration; the body takes in fresh air (oxygen) through the nose and expels waste gas (carbon dioxide), helping the metabolism of the body function smoothly. According to TCM, the lungs operate the Qi of the whole body; essence is absorbed from the universe through the nose into the lungs and spread thoughout the body.

The healing sound is Si, pronounced 'Ssssir'.

Keys points for the Lung sound

1. Make a short sharp movement and a short sharp sound.
2. Your tongue is on the top palate of your mouth with the 'sss' sound and then you quickly open your mouth with the 'ir' sound.
3. Project out with the physical movement and your awareness, to the index finger and thumb.
4. Keep your eyes open

肺经　Lung Meridian

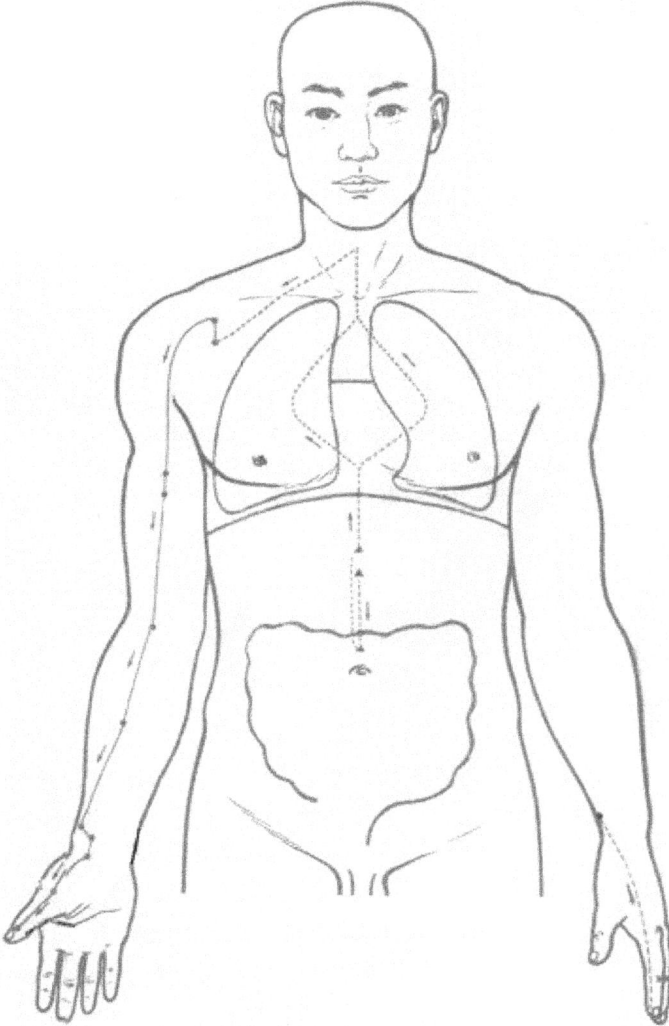

The Lung Meridian originates below the collar bone and runs down the inside of the arm to the outside of the thumb.

Section No 4. Si – Lungs

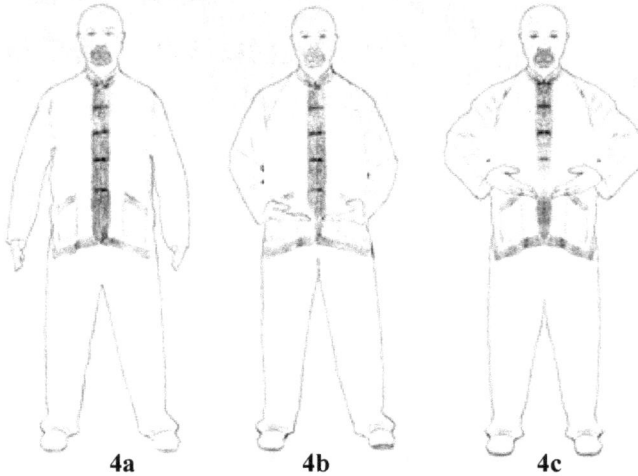

4a   **4b**   **4c**

4a-c   With your eyes closed, bring your awareness to the lungs for about ten seconds. Gently open your eyes, looking out to the distance, but not really looking. With your hands relaxed at the side of the body, keep your shoulders relaxed and gently scoop your hands in front of the body. Hold your palms facing up, as if holding a large ball in your arms at navel height (Dan Tian). Pause with one in and out breath. Breathe in and slowly raise your arms to chest height with the palms facing the sky.

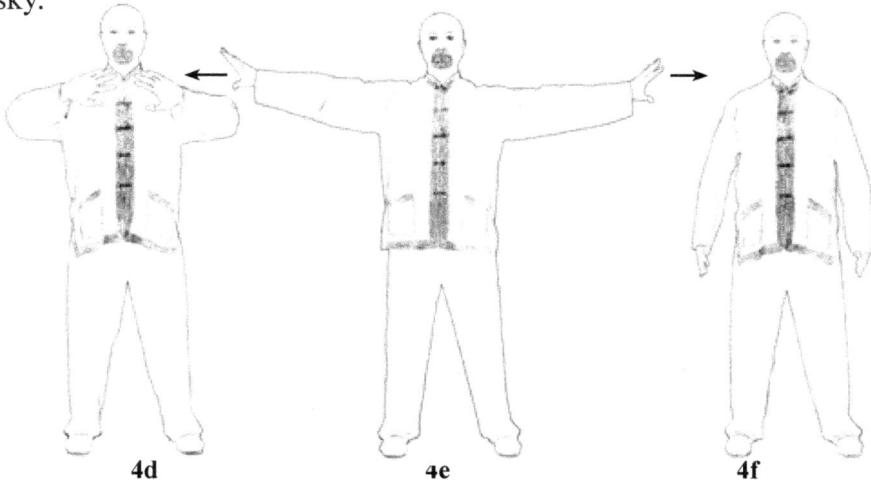

4d   **4e**   **4f**

4d-f   With your shoulders relaxed, slowly turn the hands in and rotate towards the body with your palms facing out. Breathe out the Si sound and at the same time, quickly and firmly separate the arms, pushing out to the sides of the body. Keep your hand and fingers open and using your intention, project out to the index finger and thumb. Open the chest and stimulate the Lung and Large Intestine meridian points at the tip of these fingers. Slowly allow your arms to float down to the side of your body. **Repeat for a total of six times.**

Only pause with a breath for the first movement.

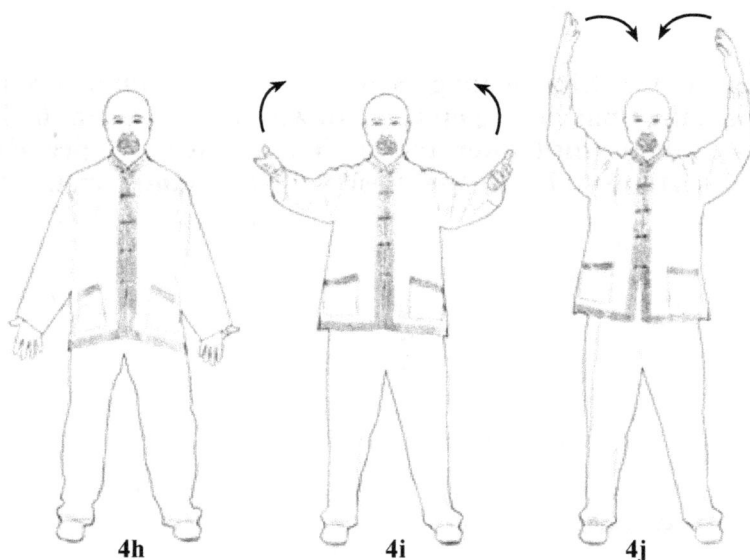

4h   4i   4j

4h-j **Closing-** Scoop your hands out, gathering the Earth Qi (Yin), then up in front of the body over the head, breathing in. Gather the Heaven Qi (Yang) to the top of the head (Bai Hui point), breathing out, and gently guiding the hands and Qi down in front of the body, palms facing down.

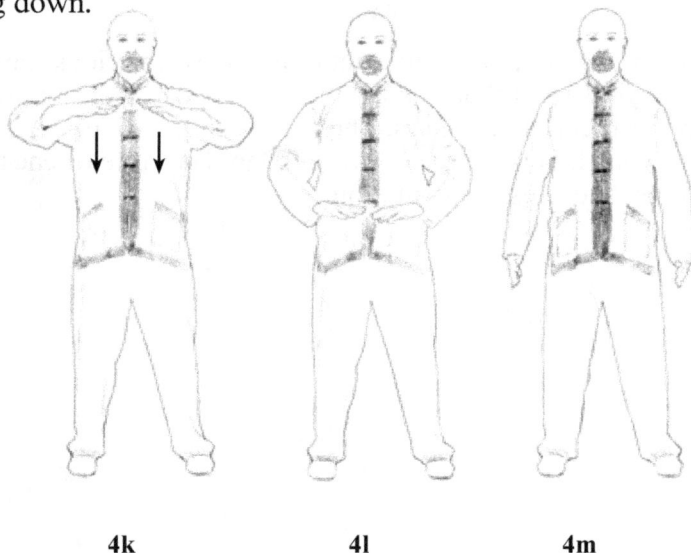

4k   4l   4m

4k-m Separate the hands as they reach the Dan Tian (navel), with fingers pointing to the ground. Allow the Heaven Qi to permeate the body both inside and out like an energy shower, cleansing and healing the whole body, to the soles of the feet to the Yong Chuan (Gushing Spring point) and into the earth. Stand with your hands relaxed at the side of your body for about 30 seconds allowing the Qi to settle; relax

If practising the Six Healing Sounds as a continuous set of movements, the final closing movement, with the hands on the Dan Tian is not done until after the sixth movement. If practising individual sections only, always close with the hands on the Dan Tian.

4n

4n   Gently move your hands in front of the body. Interlock the hands with the tip of your right thumb touching the left Lao Gong (middle of palm); relax the hands and fingers. The hands make a natural Yin/Yang shape. Place your hands over the Lower Dan Tian (area beneath the navel) and close the eyes in meditation.

Section No 5. Chui – Kidney

吹

The Water Element
Relates to the Kidney (Yin) and Bladder (Yang)

The Water Element corresponds to: the season of winter and cold weather, the direction of north, a deep blue colour and the time associated with the kidneys is 5 pm to 7 pm. The emotion that stagnates in the kidneys is fear. Yet when fear is released, the virtue of wisdom emerges.

The kidneys regulate water circulation in the body and help maintain fluid balance. In TCM the kidneys store the essence that is received from food and air which is released when the other organs require it; they are a bit like the batteries of the body. Essence is also received from our parents and is stored in the kidneys; the kidneys transform the essence into Qi or energy. It's a very important organ and it's important to keep the kidneys and the Water Element warm.

The healing sound is Chui, pronounced 'Treee'.

Keys points for the Kidney sound

1. When making the Chui sound, have a little smile at the corner of your lips.
2. Your tongue is on the lower palate of the mouth.
3. When squatting down, look straight ahead.
4. Keep eyes open

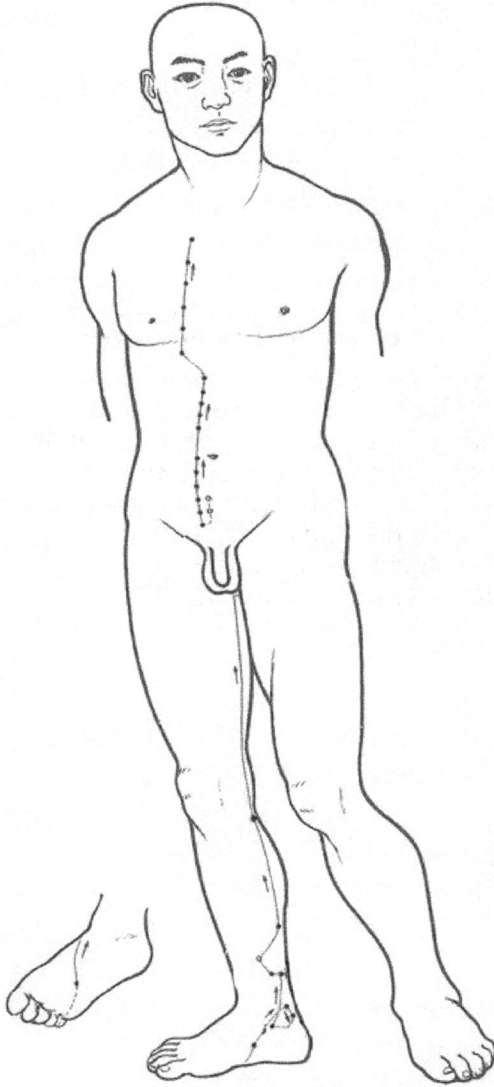

The Kidney Meridian (Y in) originates at the sole of the foot and rises up the inside of the leg, through the abdomen to the collar bone.

Section No 4. Si – Lungs

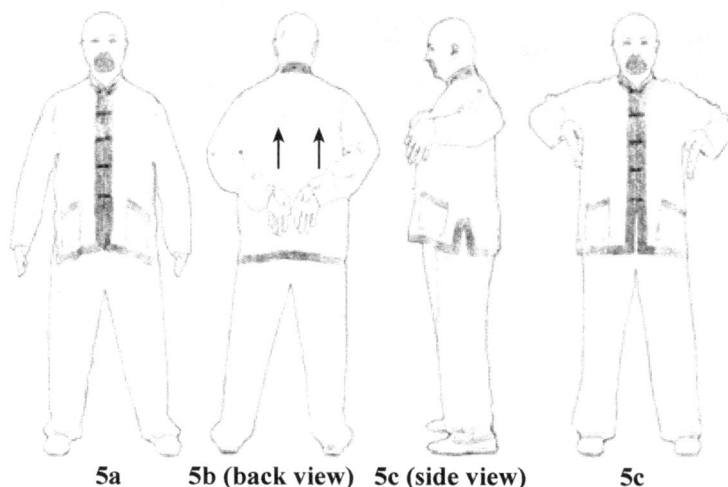

5a   5b (back view) 5c (side view)   5c

5a-c With your eyes closed, bring your awareness to the kidneys for about ten seconds. Gently open your eyes, looking out to the distance, but not really looking. With your hands relaxed at the side of the body, keep your shoulders relaxed, breathe in and gently move your arms around to the back of the body with your palms facing out over the buttocks. Slowly raise the arms with the back of your hands tracing up either side of the spine, up under the arms, keeping your shoulders relaxed and the palms facing towards the side of your chest.

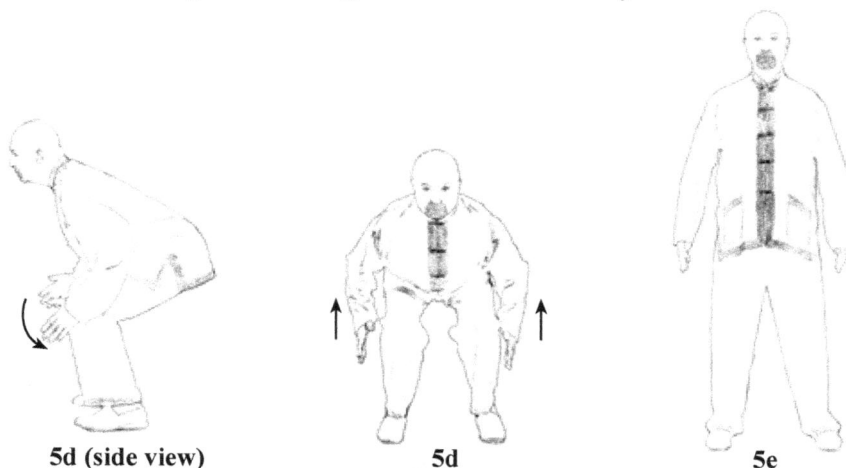

5d (side view)   5d   5e

5d-e Breathe out the Chui sound and slowly and gently bend your knees, pushing your bottom back and down as if sitting down. Keeping your head upright and looking straight ahead, the palms of your hands circle around the knee. Gently straighten your legs and return to the commencing position.
Sorry the diagrams are not showing the facial expression of the little smile. Repeat for a total of six times.

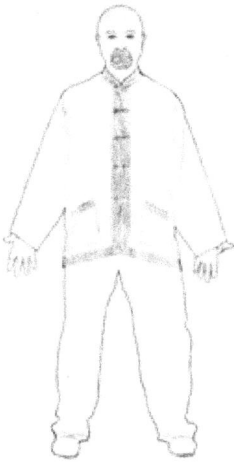  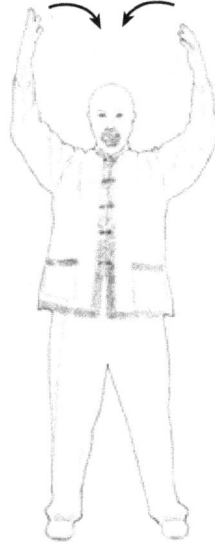

| 5f | 5g | 5h |

5f-h Closing- Scoop your hands out, gathering the Earth Qi (Yin), then lift up in front of body over the head while breathing in. Gather the Heaven Qi (Yang) to the top of the head (Bai Hui point), breathing out, and gently guide the hands and Qi down in front of the body, palms facing down.

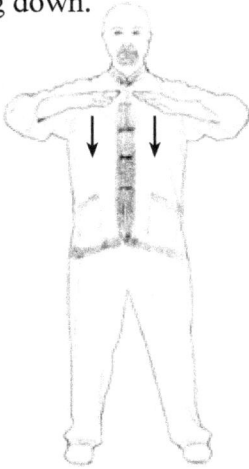 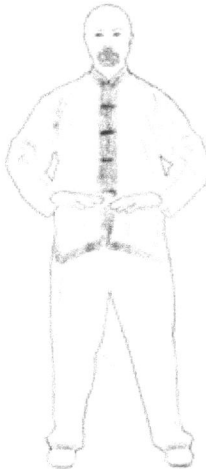 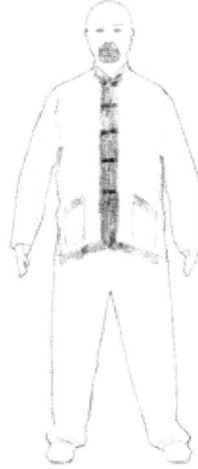

| 5i | 5j | 5k |

5i-k Separate the hands as they reach the Dan Tian (navel), with fingers pointing to the ground. Allow the Heaven Qi to permeate the body both inside and out like an energy shower, cleansing and healing the whole body, to the soles of the feet to the Yong Chuan (Gushing Spring point) and into the earth. Stand with your hands relaxed at the side of the body for about 30 seconds, allowing the Qi to settle; relax and feel.

If practising the Six Healing Sounds as a continuous set of movements, the final closing movement, with the hands on the Dan Tian is not done until after the sixth movement. If practising individual sections only, always close with the hands on the Dan Tian.

51

51 Gently move your hands in front of the body. Interlock the hands with the tip of your right thumb touching the left Lao Gong (middle of palm); relax the hands and fingers. The hands make a natural Yin/Yang shape. Place your hands over the Lower Dan Tian (area beneath the navel) and close the eyes in meditation.

Section No 6. Xi San Jiao, Triple Heater

The Fire Element
Relates to the pericardium (Yin) and San Jiao (Yang).

According to TCM, the body is divided into three sections called the 'San Jiao', which translates to the 'Triple Heater' or 'Burner'.

The Upper Heater relates to the organs above the diaphragm including the thorax, heart and lungs. The Upper Heater aids the respiratory system of the body, heats up the air and helps maintain the ability to absorb essence from the air and the universe.

The Middle Heater, located between the diaphragm and the navel, relates to the upper abdomen, the spleen, pancreas, stomach, liver, gall bladder and the small intestine. The Middle Heater functions like the oven of the body, heating the liquids and solids and aiding in their digestion. The Middle Heater promotes the absorption of essence from foods.

The Lower Heater below the navel, relates to the organs of the lower abdomen including the kidneys, bladder and large intestine. It assists in elimination from the body, also by heating up the solids and fluids.

The healing sound is Xi, pronounced 'Sheee'.

Keys points for the San Jiao sound

1. When making the Xi sound, form the mouth to make a big smile.
2. The tongue is on the lower palate of the mouth.
3. Turn the palms in towards the face when making the sound.
4. Keep eyes open

三焦经 Triple Warmer Meridian

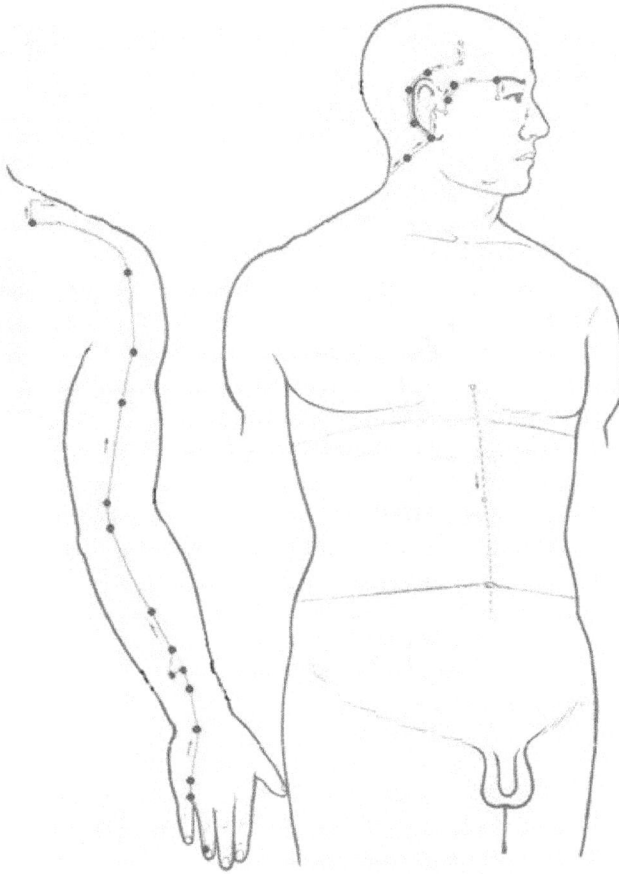

The Triple Warmer Meridian originates (Yang) starts at the tip of the ring finger, rises up the outside of the arm, the back of the shoulderto the collarbone, up the outside of the neck, and behind the ear before it dips down to the cheek and ends under the eye. An internal branch descends into the chest, through the diaphragm to the abdomen.

Section No 6. Xi San Jiao, Triple Heater

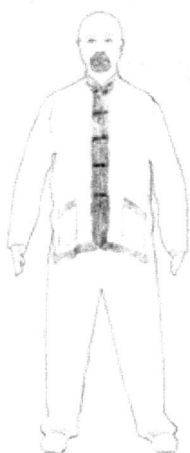  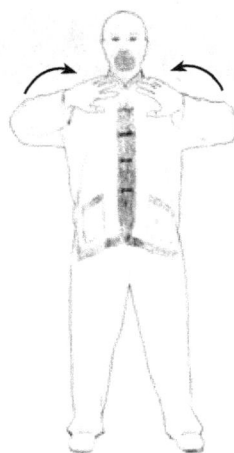

| 6a | 6b | 6c |

6a-c Your eyes are open, looking out to the distance, but not really looking. With your hands relaxed at the side of the body, keep your shoulders relaxed and gently scoop your hands in front of the body. Hold your palms facing up, as if holding a large ball in your arms at navel height (Dan Tian). Pause with one in and out breathe. Breathe in and slowly raise the hands to chest height. Turn the hands in and rotate towards the body with your palms facing out.

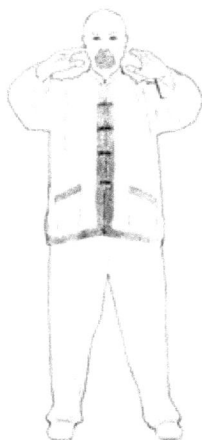  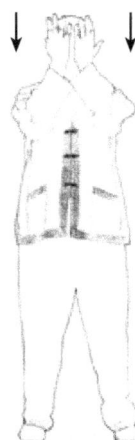

| 6d | 6e (side view) | 6e |

6d-e Breathe out the Xi sound as you move your arms away from the body with your hands in a circular shape similar to the Heart movement. Relax your shoulders and elbows and turn the palms towards the face, then slowly lower your arms with the palms tracing over the face to the chest area.

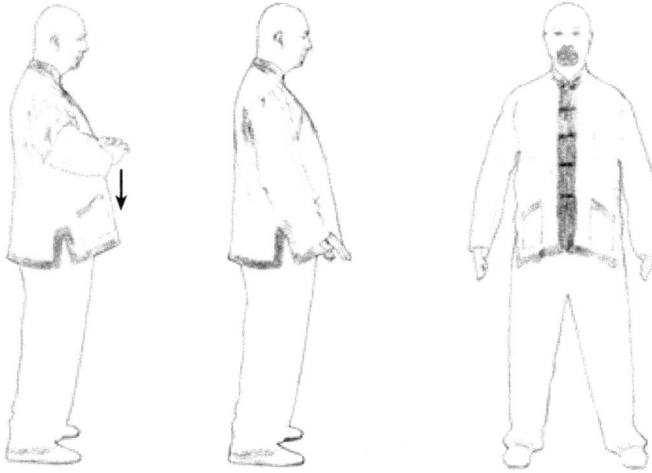

6f (side view)   **6g (side view)**   **6h**

6f-h Gently turn your palms to face the earth and slowly guide your arms and Qi down the front of the body.

Sorry the diagrams are not showing the facial expression of the big smile.

Repeat for a total of six times. Only pause with a breath for the first movement.

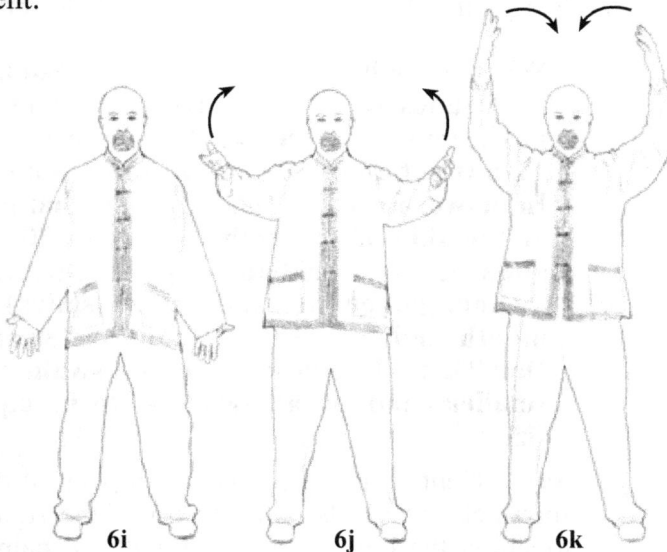

6i   **6j**   **6k**

6i-k Closing- Scoop your hands out, gathering the Earth Qi (Yin), then lift up in front of the body over the head, breathing in. Gather the Heaven Qi (Yang) to the top of the head (Bai Hui point), breathing out, and gently guide the hands and Qi down in front of the body, palms facing down.

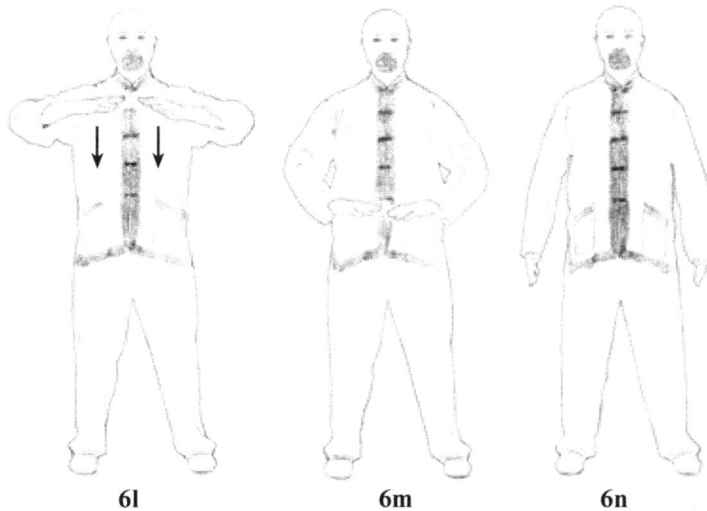

6l	**6m**	**6n**

6l-n   Separate the hands as they reach the Dan Tian (navel), with fingers pointing to the ground. Allow the Heaven Qi to permeate the body both inside and out like an energy shower, cleansing and healing the whole body, to the soles of the feet to the Yong Chuan (Gushing Spring point) and into the earth. Stand with your hands relaxed at the side of your body for about 30 seconds, allowing the Qi to settle; relax and feel.

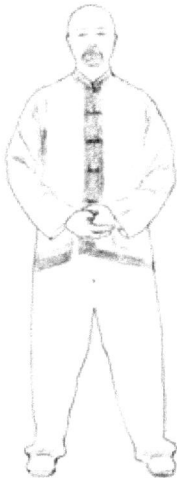

6o

When practising the Six Healing Sounds as a continuous set of movements, the final closing movement with the hands on the Lower Dan Tian is not done until after the sixth movement. In between each section, allow the hands to rest at the side of the body for about 30 seconds, allowing the meridian to open. After the sixth section, gather the Jade Nectar (saliva) in your mouth and take three meditative swallows to Dan Tian. Making sure the first swallow is a bit smaller enabling all swallows to be equally in size.

6o   Gently move your hands in front of the body. Interlock the hands with the tip of the right thumb touching the left Lao Gong (middle of palm); relax the hands and fingers. The hands make a natural Yin/Yang shape. Place your hands over the Lower Dan Tian (area beneath the navel) and close the eyes in meditation.

Section No 7 - Closing and Processing the Qi

After purging and cleansing the organ meridians of the body with the Six Healing Sounds, we finish by bringing positive healing energy back into our bodies. We gently rub our hands together, bringing our healing energy, love and kindness through the heart and into our hands. Then place our warm healing hands over each organ for about 30 seconds, allowing it to absorb the healing Qi energy. Finish with a fifteen minute sitting meditation in what we call the 'processing stage'. When the body comes to a complete stop, the Qi keeps moving and through the tranquillity of the mind the Qi will come into balance.

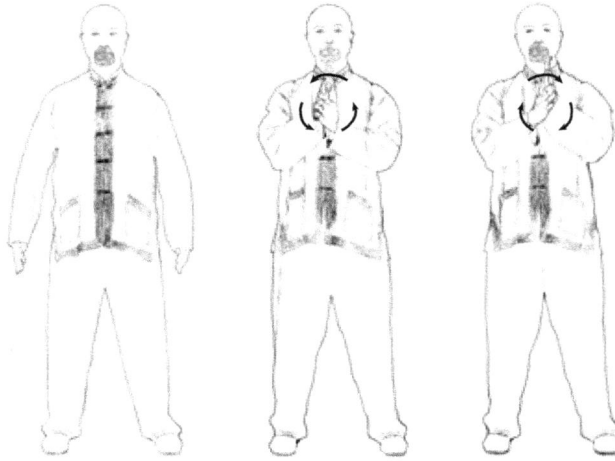

7a   7b   7c

7a-c   Start to gently rub the hands together, bringing healing energy, love and kindness through the heart into your hands. Gently rub your hands for about 60 seconds allowing them to become warm and soft.

7d	**7e**	**7f**

7d-f Now, place these warm healing hands over the liver on your right hand side next to the heart. Allow the liver to absorb the warmth; the healing Qi. Then place your palms over the heart and allow the heart to absorb the warm healing Qi. Now the spleen on the left hand side of the body; relax and feel.

7g	**7h (back view)**	**7i**

7g-i Now place both palms over both lungs across the chest, allowing your lungs to absorb the Qi. Then place both palms over the kidneys, allowing the kidneys to absorb the warm healing Qi; relax and feel. Gently move your hands in front of the body. Interlock the hands, making a natural Yin/Yang shape. Place your hands over the Lower Dan Tian (area beneath the navel) and close the eyes in meditation.

7j (side view) **7k** **7l**

7j-l The final stage is ideally 15 minutes of meditation, either sitting cross-legged on the floor or on the edge of a chair keeping the back straight. The chin is tucked in, with the tip of the tongue on the top palate of the mouth, just behind the teeth. Breathe naturally in and out through the nose. Sense the breath and sense the peace. Allow the breath to become smooth and even and the mind to rest for at least five minutes.

Turn the hands in over the Dan Tian, the area beneath the navel, with one hand on top of the other. Allow your mind, breath and energy to settle. When breathing in, the abdomen gently pushes out into your hands. When breathing out it gently push the hands in. Relax and feel the whole body breathe for another five minutes.

Place the hands with palms down on the knees sensing the inner peace. Through the peace, allow the heart to open like a smile, with a wave of loving kindness permeating from the heart through the whole body. Just relax and let it go out through every cell. Every cell of the body is smiling with the radiance of the universe as you become one with the universe for another five minutes.

12.74 p

Thank you.
谢谢

Chapter 6
Stories to Inspire

Six Healing Sounds
Nurturing Life Qigong

Stories to Inspire

I have been learning Tai Chi and Qigong for the last 12 years but have moved to practising Qigong more over the last four years. I practise Qigong for half an hour, four or five mornings a week, as well as teaching for three hours a week.

I began practising Qigong because I have severe Rheumatoid Arthritis and I was looking for something that would assist me in managing this condition. Once I began learning about medical Qigong, I liked how the moves linked to the organs in the body, as well as the different meridians. I also felt better in myself after practising and could feel myself getting rid of stale Qi and taking in fresh Qi, especially when I linked the movements to my breathing. I also like the way it links everything to nature.

I became interested in the Six Healing Sounds because I regularly attend meditations, where sound is used to enhance the meditation process. I have also been involved in some sound healing sessions and have felt the effects sound can have on shifting blockages and altering our brainwave state.

My research as a teacher trainer and teaching Early Childhood students how best to work with young children from birth onwards, has shown me the importance of sounds, singing and music in all aspects of learning and life right throughout the lifespan. We can't underestimate the importance sounds and music has for all of us.

I find the combination of movements, sound and knowing what area of the body we are focusing on to be very powerful. Combining sound with particular movements excites me as it means we are further enhancing the effect Qigong has. I find combining sound with the Qigong movements really enhances the experience.

Qigong is where movements are done to stimulate the Qi and in so doing, allowing the Qi to move to where it needs to go, to bring about healing and a sense of wellbeing. Medical Qigong stimulates the meridians and focuses Qi on particular organs of the body. It is a very old form of Chinese healing. When the moves are coupled with breathing, the feeling intensifies and the benefits are greater.

After I have practised Qigong I feel calmer and more relaxed and I can feel the tension in my body being dispersed. I also have a strong sense of wellbeing after practising Qigong. At times I feel the Qi, especially in my hands, when I practise certain moves.

The other thing I have found really helpful is the way Master Simon pauses for a little while after some moves. I first experienced this in one of Master Simon's weekend workshops and from then on I was 'hooked' on his type of medical Qigong.

For me, the benefits of Qigong practice are that my joints are being regularly exercised and maintain flexibility, Qi is being stimulated and I feel a strong sense of calm and wellbeing. Through doing this I have been able to put off having to have further joint repairing operations.

The hand surgeon I consulted for my severely deformed hands was surprised at how much movement I have in my wrists, given the damage that has been done there. I put that down directly to some of the movements that we do in the warm-ups as well as the some of the wrist movements done in Qigong.

I have learned that if I practise Qigong regularly it does have a profound effect on my sense of wellbeing as well as my general health. I have tried to bring the different ways of breathing into other aspects of my life to calm myself down and also to help me get to sleep. I also get a great kick out of others becoming aware of their Qi in my classes and being excited about that. **Adrienne**

I have been practising Qigong, Tai Chi and meditation for over 25 years. I started when I was quite young and very ill, drawn to the gentle approach to practice and facinated by the Chinese healing arts. In only my second class I felt the Qi burning in my palms and I have been hooked ever since. After 10 years of being a student I beame an instructor, although I think you remain a student for life.

When I first started practising the Six Healing Sounds I was amazed at how such a subtle practice could be so powerful. How different ways of using the sounds can have different effects in the body. As with many practices, 'more' (or louder) is not always best. With intention and correct practice, the softest, quietest sound can have the most impact on your energy and emotions.

In my experience practising and teaching the Six Healing Sounds, the results are amazing and varied. Depending on the person, their intention, the quality of their practice and just where they are at on the day, what they experience is different evrything from irritability, discomfort and revealed emotions to deep relaxation, clear and calm. I love how you can use it any way you need at the time and how it brings you closer to your authentic self. It's hard to put into words you can only understand how it will work for you by doing it yourself. **Elizabeth**

I have been practising Qigong for almost two years and rarely miss the weekly class. I have a busy lifestyle so my frequency of practice depends very much on what else is happening around me at the time.

If I am busy I may only practise once a week, perhaps a couple of times, sometimes never, except in class. I have found that the more I practise the more I WANT to practise. It seems to have that effect on me, so if I am on a roll I try and stay there!

I started practising Qigong because I was looking for a method of exercise that would be low impact, but at the same time stimulating and enjoyable. I had tried yoga but had to give that away as my arthritic hand and wrist joints could not handle the floor work, which meant I was sitting around a lot of the time doing nothing. When I saw a notice about Qigong classes in my area I was immediately intrigued and interested, so I made enquiries.

I understand the principles of Qigong but have not taken the time to study the theory in detail. I would love to learn more, however there are never enough hours in the day for everything I need and want to do, so any new commitment has to be on the 'wish' list for the time being.ng is wonderful! I feel more supple and agile physically and am much calmer and settled in myself.

I used to get stressed under pressure, and abrupt and frustrated if things didn't go my way. Now I find these little annoyances in life are just that, 'little'. I am more laid back in everything I do and can take things in my stride.

It's good having an interest strong enough to take me out of my usual routine, in which I was previously always too busy to commit to outside activities. I've learned that the simple things in life can sometimes give the most pleasure. It is possible to feel calm and contented in a world that is quite the opposite. **Gay**

I have been practising Qigong since 2001, three times a week on average.

I started practising Qigong and the Chinese healing arts when I had a serious health crisis in 2000. I had chronic fatigue and multiple chemical sensitivity with liver and kidney complications.

Along with Qigong I also use Chinese massage and occasionally acupuncture. I follow a Buddhist practice that also works with mantra vibrations as a healing tool, thus I find the Six Healing Sounds complementary and gentle, yet powerful within.

Qigong to me is life-affirming. It's a modality that enhances and invigorates the body and mind's energetic system so it can self-regulate. Each body has its own needs for healthy living. By doing

Qigong movements and meditation, one's body absorbs and interprets what it requires to adjust and heal itself with no force, no real strain, just gentle awareness and doing.

Regular Qigong moving practice and Qi meditation makes me aware and connected to my body in everyday activities, by understanding its needs. Qi meditation calms and focuses my mind, so there is less stress, less worry and more possibility of enjoying life. The healing sounds are interesting to me as they bring more attention and care to these unseen aspects of our bodies.

I've had many benefits from practising Qigong. My fatigue has lifted and I have good physical vitality. My kidney and liver energies are much improved and my immune system has improved while I continue to look after myself.

The meditative, still and concentration aspects of Qigong ('quietness within movement' and 'nothingness' meditation), has given me space and calm to see my own and others' actions more gently, allowing me to relax into what is bushfire or party time! **Glenda**

I've been practising Qigong for about 15 years, generally at least four times a week and I also teach twice a week.

I was introduced to Qigong by a friend who was in the same meditation group. My husband and I joined Simon's class and I immediately connected with the practice.

I love anything to do with sound! I was particularly interested in how sound can heal. I love singing and chanting and the effects they had, so it was a natural progression that the Six Healing Sounds would be effective.

I see Qigong as a form of energy work that is self-healing, with a spiritual aspect too. The exercises are designed to unblock the acupuncture meridians, or channels, so the Qi can flow smoothly through the body.

It makes me feel very relaxed with a calm mind and it has a profound effect on my energy very quickly. It keeps my joints free, regulates all the systems of the body and keeps me 'in tune'.

I've learned that even when life can turn upside down, we can remain calm and in control of our emotions. As a teacher of Qigong, being able to share the benefits is particularly rewarding.

Thanks Simon for sharing your passion. It is evident in your teaching skills that you are a true master! **Jaye**

I practise Qigong four times a week. I started because I had read about Qigong and the flow of energy and the healing aspects and thought it would be good for me.

I really love doing the Six Healing Sounds because I can feel that the area concerned is benefiting from the practice.

I think that Qigong is a number of practices that help with the flow of 'Qi' around the body. By Qi, my understanding is the energy flow. After doing the practices I can always feel the energy in my body, especially in my hands as I move them together and then apart.

Qigong makes me feel calm and consequently helps in my relationships. It makes me feel as if I am actively doing something for my health that doesn't require others, but is a personal practice.

When I practise Qigong, one of the benefits is that I am less likely to react to what is happening around me. To be able to do this helps me cope with life a lot better than when I didn't do Qigong. I have learned that when I am practising Qigong, life takes on a more rosy aspect. The everyday news about violence and killings become less threatening as I am able to remain calm.

Thank you Simon for opening this practice up for me. It has become a real lifesaver and a place for me to retreat into to remain calm in the hurly-burly of life around me. It is a real blessing that you came into my life. **Lesley**

I have been practising a mixture of Tai Chi and Qigong for about 21 years. I practise regularly once a week, but if learning a new form or reviewing a form, it will be a lot more often.

I started practising when I was a working mother. I was looking for something just for me. I have practised a number of different Qigong forms and had done some healing sounds but not with movements, until I went on a retreat with Simon.

I enjoyed the combination of moving with the deep breathing and sounds. I found doing this seemed to generate quite a bit of warmth and the placing of the hands on the respective organ areas while following the sounds felt really good.

Qigong to me is moving meditation. It focuses my mind on what my body is doing and at the same time it is gently stretching and moving all of my joints and muscles.

Once I know the moves of the form and don't have to concentrate on what comes next, it makes me feel warm, relaxed and calm. Doing Qigong helps keep my back free of stiffness and is great for keeping muscles and joints loose and active. It also helps with my balance and keeps my mind active. I've learned that it is now easier to let go of a hectic day and to relax doing something I enjoy and benefit from. **Linda**

We've been practising Qigong for two years, five days per week.

We have done some vibrational sound therapy and other Chinese healing arts, combined with a spiritual practice and a lifestyle of peace and harmony. We enjoy Simon Blow's teaching method of loving kindness and his generosity in sharing the ancient knowledge passed down from his lineage of Chinese teachers.

Qigong is a balance of Qi, Yin and Yang and brings the essence of Dao through body movement awareness, to embody universal harmony and a peaceful way for all beings.

Qigong makes us feel tranquil and calm with an awareness of the deep breath of life. Also the practice gives us a calm basis to face the adversities of human society in a peaceful and loving manner.

Qigong harmonises the whole body, mind and spirit and gives us a tranquil emotional and spiritual grounding for each moment in the day. The more we slow down, the more we become aware and awake to life's journey and can feel the Qi flowing from the universal source through our bodies.

Simon has reinforced our journey's validity and importance through his own life. Qigong has given us a gentle and yet deeply powerful physical practice to balance our spiritual meditation. As a result we feel much more grounded, clear and centred in the Dao of universal love. Thank you Simon and the teachers who have been so generous to share this with all of us.

Margarite's poem: *With every breath comes a new spark of light upon the earth, we ground and hold the deep essence of Life.* **Margarite and Mark**

I've been practising Qigong for three to four years and I try to do it daily.

A yoga friend suggested I might enjoy it, so I went to a little local group where I loved it. As I've always enjoyed yoga, ballet and dance, the beautiful slow movements just touched a spot in my being that felt like home. That was it. My yoga practice has been in place for 30 odd years, however Qigong now plays the most important role in my life.

I've had two years of serious illness but I am now feeling great. I love how the Six Healing Sounds sends vibrations through the various organs of my body. It makes me feel good. If I concentrate on the vibration as I make the sound, I feel sometimes that I can remove the hindrance in that organ.

Qigong is an ancient Chinese art form that heals the body, mind, soul and spirit. I guess it's about finding a peace or a nothingness. It's about breathing and feeling the energy (Qi). It may also improve health and cure some illnesses. It makes me feel peaceful, energised and happy. It helps with my spiritual growth, meditating more deeply, fitness and joy. Also, I'm learning about my weaknesses and attitudes.

Unlike any other thing that I have done, Qigong is important to me. It's like coming home. **Sandy**

I've been practising Qigong for about 18 years and I practise most days. Sometimes it's just as simple as sitting still and concentrating on bringing awareness to the breath.

I was searching for something as a child and when I came across Qigong in my twenties I wasn't ready. I didn't start practising until my thirties when it felt right and just resonated.

I practised something similar about 15 years ago and always liked the link with the sounds, particular organs and elements. This form goes into so much depth, like season and colour, which I find awesome.

For me Qigong is movement, focus and breathing. By this I mean moving your energy mentally and physically so it flows, focusing on your mental state which calms and clears the mind leading to awareness that's like meditation, and concentrating on your abdominal breathing.

Qigong makes me feel calmer and I find practice always puts a smile on my face. I'm typically a high-energy person, always on the go, so I find Qigong helps me find balance (Yin and Yang). I also find I think clearer and have more compassion.

Life is about balance. Too much Qi or not enough can affect your mental, physical and emotional stability. I also like being able to play with my Qi energy and getting it to flow.

I love being able to practise after tea each night, as I find I can build up stress unwittingly throughout the day, but I would recommend practising the Six Healing Sounds at the time it resonates with you. On my bucket list is to one day practise Six Healing Sounds high on a mountain sitting on a rock, at sunset! **Suse**

I've been practising Qigong for nearly 18 years and I practise most days.

A diagnosis of osteoporosis and osteoarthritis 18 years ago, made me decide to find a way of helping myself, rather than turning to medications with harmful side effects.

I also use acupressure on myself, meditation and have had several acupuncture treatments reinforced with the use of Chinese herbs.

Qigong is for me an energy cultivation which allows me to be a stronger and better person. It gives me more understanding of the world about me and my place in it.

It makes me feel calmer and more in control of my emotions, particularly negative ones, and fills me with quiet inner peace.

It has strengthened my body and made it more flexible, allowing me to deal with my headaches and migraines more easily and mostly without medication. It has made me a more balanced person.

It has taught me to be a more compassionate person and a more self-confident being. It has taught me to leave painful experiences behind, to live more in the present and not to worry too much about the future.

The world would be such a better place if everybody was practising Qigong. We would live longer without putting so much stress on medical resources. We would be much healthier and happier! **Sylvie**

I've been practising Qigong since 1994, about four to five times per week.

I started because I had just been diagnosed with Multiple Sclerosis (MS) and needed some form of exercise to maintain muscle tone. My Tai Chi teacher said that Qigong would help best. I also have acupuncture regularly and have taken Chinese herbs.

I see Qigong as a form of exercise that transcends the physical and promotes the movement of energy and Qi throughout the body. It enhances balance and wellbeing, while maintaining muscle tone. Better still, Qigong, unlike aerobic exercise, is all within my capability, despite having physical limits due to having MS.

I am still walking while many of my acquaintances with MS are deteriorating. It gives me a feeling of wellbeing when I am feeling unwell from the MS.

It gives me the energy to get moving in the morning when my limbs are not cooperating. The physical improvement gives me a feeling of capability and the possibility that I can do movements, which otherwise I would not be able to do. It makes me feel whole again for a while.

It's essential to practise regularly, always with the awareness that the practice helps develop better health and wellbeing. It is also important to find the particular forms that benefit the individual and to practise them at the appropriate times, so they can provide the benefit needed in that moment. I recommend the practice of Qigong to all. But, especially to those who have health and movement issues. **Vanessa**

I've been practising Qigong for about two years and my goal is to practise early each morning, but I'm not always successful. However, when I do, I find it is a wonderful start to the day.

I had been doing yoga for years, but following illness and a couple of operations, I found it was a bit too strenuous. Qigong is just perfect for me now. I love the gentle, flowing movements which put me in a wonderfully meditative space, enhanced enormously by Simon's DVDs.

As I've become older I am drawn more to meditation, toning and the power of sound for healing. I have a love of ancient celadons and Chinese philosophy and I value the references to Chinese philosophers in your books.

I see Qigong as a gentle, holistic method of exercise which is beneficial for my health, breathing, meditation and spirituality.

When I practise, I feel relaxed and more aware. It has taught me to appreciate the value of being in the now and of surrender and acceptance. Also about the beauty and magic of nature and the joy of living simply and fully.

The benefits for me are in having a richer quality of life and increased perception and enjoyment of nature. I'm more conscious of what I eat because I'm listening to my body more, so I'm able to take responsibility for my own health. I'm allowing my inner voice to guide me and following that momentum, rather than the mind, which can set up needless fears and obstacles.

I really connect with Simon's approach and style as a teacher. I'm so appreciative that the universe (as always) found him for me. It was perfect timing. **Zoe**

I've been practising Qigong for one year, about once or twice a week. I was first taught some at a health retreat and loved it. It made me feel so calm. I've also tried acupressure and cupping techniques.

I think of Qigong as a moving meditation, or concentrating the Qi to assist with healing. It makes me feel relaxed and in touch with Gaia and the universe.

It's helped with calming and quietening my overactive mind and there's a feeling of calmness when practising it. I'm able to feel that I'm in the here and now and not worrying about the future or the outside world: at least for a while. I've learned it's OK to go within, the outside world doesn't always need me there.

I've also learned how to incorporate some of the Qigong into my Pilates teaching, especially the warm-ups. **Stephani**

Recently I have practised Qigong daily at least twice, sometimes three times.

I feel very calm, integrated and clear after practice. I find when I combine 'nothingness' meditation, I feel my life flows and a synchronicity of issues occurs naturally. I also notice I have more natural mobility in my right wrist and am able to move my thumb and index fingers more freely.

With considerable intention, I've found the Six Healing Sounds to have a very distinct detoxification effect on the specific organs of practice. I've also felt stagnant Qi dispersing and an absorbing Qi flow in the organs and meridians of the body. One feels calm and clear.

I am grateful to have you as my teacher. You have a very deep experiential understanding of Qigong and a sincere nature. You teach and impart the art form to your students in a simple and practical manner, helping them learn to the best of their capacity with clarity and correct form. **Arthur**

I have been practising Qigong for 12 months; I go to one class a week and then practise at home for an average of 30 minutes a day.

I had an accident three years ago and fractured my spine in four places and damaged my stomach. I am on an enteral feeding pump for 16 hours a day and have a lot of neck and back pain. I also suffer from post-traumatic stress disorder following severe abuse. Thus, I was afraid to be connected to my body.

I started Qigong because I wanted to find a gentle and safe way to reconnect to my body, release locked emotions and improve my digestion and mobility. I was drawn to the Six Healing Sounds Qigong as I needed to verbally express my sadness and anger about my abuse.

Qigong makes me feel grounded, centered, empowered and vital. Other benefits have been: increased absorption and better digestion, increased mobility, increased energy and a deeper connection to mind, body and spirit. Sometimes I feel quite emotional, as I release things that I have been holding onto.

I have learned how much I hold onto emotions, rather than expressing them and how this impacts my body. Also, how profound gentle movement such as Qigong can be.

Simon has a special gift of presence and spiritual connection, so I always feel safe to allow my body to do whatever it needs to do, in order to balance mind, body and spirit.

I love Simon's books and DVDs. They have given me a better understanding of what the Qigong movements are doing to aid my body. I use the DVDs daily, so that I can continue my practice at home.

I am loving the Six Healing Sounds, as adding the sounds as a way of cleansing the organs really works for me, and is also a way of releasing emotions. I tend to hold onto anger and as a result, I have a lot of inflammatory conditions. Now I can use the Six Healing Sounds to express myself and enhance my liver, which is most affected by anger.

When I began Qigong 12 months ago, I had to sit through the whole class. Now I can stand for the whole time. Twelve months ago, I could only walk for 15 minutes and then the back pain was too severe to continue. Now I can walk on the beach for two hours a day. I am so grateful for Simon, the Qigong and Simon's books and DVDs. They have brought me back to life. **Jayne**

CDs – by Simon Blow

CD1: Five Elements Qigong Meditation

This CD is the perfect introduction to Qigong meditation (Neigong). **Track one** features a 30-minute heart-felt guided meditation to help bring love and light from the universe into your body. It harmonises the Five Elements – Fire, Earth, Metal, Water and Wood – with the corresponding organs of the body, respectively the heart, spleen, lungs, kidney and liver. This is one of the foundations of Chinese Qigong. Let Qigong Master Simon Blow help harmonise the elements of the universe with the energy of your body by using colour and positive images. **Track two** provides 30 minutes of relaxing music by inspiring composer Dale Nougher.

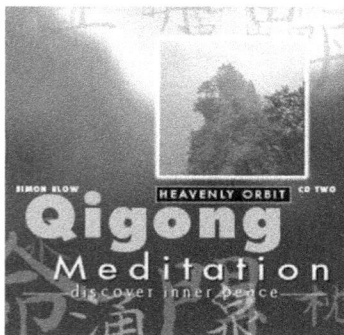

CD2: Heavenly Orbit Qigong Meditation

This CD is intended for the intermediate student. **Track one** takes you through a 30-minute guided meditation using your awareness to stimulate the energy centres around the body and open all the meridians. The circulation of Qi (Chi) around the Heavenly Orbit is one of the foundations of Chinese Qigong. The energy rising up the back 'Du' channel harmonises with the energy descending down the front 'Ren' channel, helping balance the energy of the body. Master Simon Blow guides you to open the energy centres of your own body to create harmony with the universe. **Track two** provides 30 minutes of relaxing music by Dale Nougher.

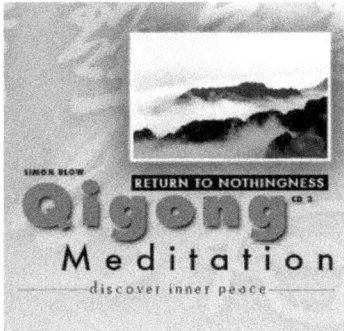

CD3: Return to Nothingness Qigong Meditation

This CD is intended for the advanced student and those wanting a healing night-practice. One of the aims of Qigong is to allow our internal energy (Qi) to harmonise with the external energy (Qi) allowing our consciousness to merge with the universe. When we enter into a deep sleep or meditation all the meridians start to open and much healing can take place. In this 20-minute guided meditation Simon Blow assists you in guiding your energy through your body and harmonising with the energy of the universe. Track two provides 30 minutes of healing music by Dale Nougher.

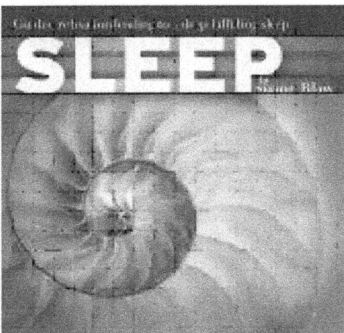

Sleep

Sleep is necessary to maintain life, alongside breathing, eating, drinking, and exercising of the mind and body. Without a good six to eight hours of sleep each night it can be hard to live a quality, balanced, fulfilling life. When we sleep it's a time to rest and rejuvenate the mind and body and to release the physical, mental and emotional stress that has built up during the day. This also helps uplift us spiritually.

It's a time to rest; it's time for a good night's sleep. Let Simon Blow's soothing voice, along with Dale Nougher's beautiful piano music and the natural sounds of the ocean, help guide you to release the tension of the day and enable you to enter a deep, fulfilling sleep.

Book/DVD sets – by Simon Blow

"About 18 months ago I started to practise Qigong as I knew that it would improve my health. I needed to do it regularly, ideally every day, but being in a rural area presented logistical problems. I discovered Simon's DVD and commenced daily practice. The great advantage for me was that I didn't have to travel to classes and could do them whenever I felt like it. Since that time I have noticed great improvement in my overall wellbeing. It has helped me to reinvent my clinical practice as a holistic massage practitioner. A number of my clients now have Simon's DVD and I feel this is helping them to both improve their health and well being, and to empower themselves." **Robin Godson-King (Holistic Massage Practitioner)**

(Each set contains a DVD plus a book that provides diagrams and instructions for the movements contained on the DVD. The book also includes interesting reading about the practice of Qigong as well as inspirational stories.)

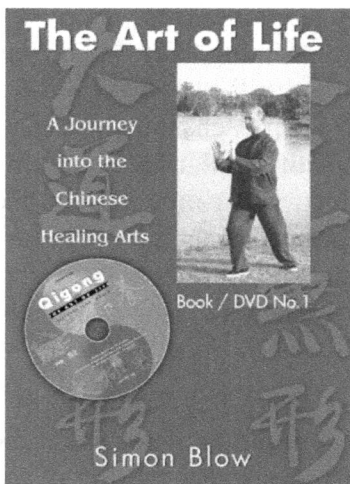

The Art of Life

'The Art of Life' presents the Qigong styles that were taught to me in Australia: the Taiji Qigong Shibashi, which I learned as an instructor with the Australian Academy of Tai Chi from 1990 to 1995; and the Ba Duan Jin standing form, commonly known as the Eight Pieces of Brocade, taught to me in 1996 by Sifu John Dolic in Sydney.

This is the perfect introduction to this ancient art and is suitable for new and continuing students of all ages. The book follows the DVD and contains three sections: **1. Warm up** – gentle movements loosen all the major joints of the body, lubricating the tendons and helping increase blood and energy circulation. It is beneficial for most arthritic conditions; **2. Ba Duan Jin or Eight Pieces of Brocade** – this is the best known and most widely practised form of Qigong throughout the world, also known as Daoist Yoga. The movements stretch all the major muscles, massage organs and open the meridians of the body; **3. Taiji Qigong Shibashi** – this popular practice is made up of eighteen flowing movements. The gentle movements harmonise the mind, body and breath. Total running time: 55 minutes.

"Tai Chi Qigong is a gentle way of exercising the whole body and provides long-term benefits. I recommend it to my patients as an effective way of improving muscle tone and joint mobility. Those who practise regularly have fewer problems with their muscles and joints and often report an increased sense of health and wellbeing. This is an excellent video with clear and simple instruction."
Roman Maslak. B.A. (Hons), D.O. Osteopath

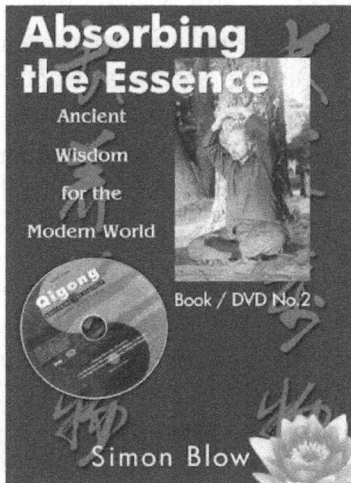

Absorbing the Essence

'Absorbing the Essence' comprises the Qigong cultivation techniques that were taught to me by Grand Master Zhong Yunlong in 1999 and 2000 at Wudangshan or Wudang Mountain. Wudang is one of the sacred Daoist Mountains of China and is renowned for the development of Taiji.

This DVD and book is for the intermediate student and for people with experience in meditation. It contains three sections: **1. Warm up** – the same as in The Art of Life DVD; **2. Wudang Longevity Qigong** – this sequence of gentle, flowing movements stimulates the Heavenly Orbit, absorbing the primordial energy from the environment and letting the negativity dissolve into the distance; **3. Sitting Ba Duan Jin** – this 30-minute sequence includes eight sections with exercises to stimulate different organs and meridians of the body. It is practised in a seated position on a chair or cushion – ideal for people who have discomfort whilst standing. These practices originated from the famous Purple Cloud Monastery at the sacred Wudang Mountain in China. Total running time: 60 minutes.

"Simon Blow of Australia has twice travelled (1999, 2000) to Mt Wudang Shan Daoist Wushu College to learn Taiji Hunyuan Zhuang (Longevity) Qigong and Badajin Nurturing Life Qigong and through his study has absorbed the essence of these teachings. Therefore, I specially grant Simon the authority to teach these, spreading the knowledge of these Qigong methods he has learnt at Mt Wudang to contribute to the wellbeing of the human race. May the Meritorious Deeds Be Infinite."
Grand Master Zhong Yunlong, Daoist Priest and Director,
Mt Wudang Shan Taoist Wushu College, China, September 24, 2000.

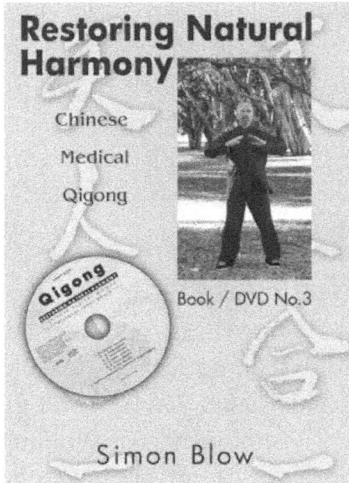

Restoring Natural Harmony

This DVD and book is for the advanced student or for the person wanting to learn specific Traditional Chinese Medicine self-healing exercises. Each section works on a different organ meridian system of the body – Spleen, Lungs, Kidney, Liver and Heart – which relate to the Five Elements – Earth, Metal, Water, Wood and Fire. Guigen Qigong originated from Dr Xu Hongtao, a Qigong Specialist Doctor from the Xiyuan Hospital in Beijing. These internal exercises help regulate the meridian system bringing harmony to mind, body and spirit. Total running time: 75 minutes.

"Simon Blow first visited our hospital in 2002. I was impressed with his knowledge and commitment to Qigong. He returned in 2004 to study Chinese Medical Qigong. Simon is a gifted teacher: he has the rare ability to inspire others and impart to them the healing benefits of Qigong."
Dr Xu Hongtao, Qigong and Tuina Department, Xiyuan Hospital Beijing, China.

"This DVD – the third by the impressively qualified Sydney-based Simon Blow – serves two purposes. Firstly, it is so attractively produced that the curious would surely be induced to investigate further. Secondly, for those already practising, it provides a mnemonic device much more useful than a series of still pictures." **Review by Adyar Bookshop, Sydney 2005.**

These are not medical devices and should not be used to replace any existing medical treatment. Always consult with your health provider if uncertain.

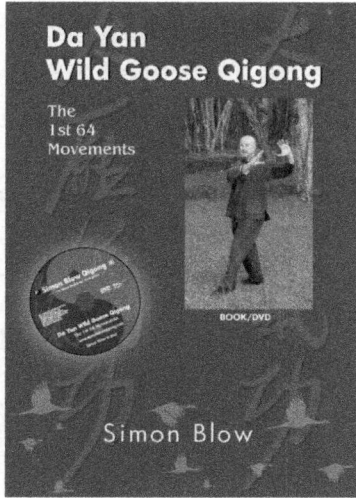

Da Yan Wild Goose Qigong
The first 64 movements

'Da Yan' translates to 'great bird' and is an ancient cultivation practice originating from the Jin Dynasty about 1700 years ago. Daoist Masters from the sacred Kunlun Mountains, in the Northern Himalayan area in south-west China, would observe the migrating geese which descended in this area each year. They would mimic the movements of these great birds and started to developed the Da Yan Wild Goose Qigong system.

Its healing and spiritual legacy was passed down through many generations; however Dayan Qigong was withheld from the general public until 1978. Then 27th lineage holder Grand Master Yang Mei Jung (1895-2002) decided to teach this ancient Qigong practice and share its healing benefits to improve the quality of life of all people.

The 1st 64 movement set deals primary with the 'post-natal body' relating to the energy that one gathers after birth. The movements representing the flight of wild geese are slow, graceful movements and strong, quick movements designed to release stale Qi and to gather fresh Qi, helping to restore balance and stimulate the entire energy system of the body.

'I've benefitted in many ways from Qigong. In physical terms, I'm stronger, have better balance and coordination and my muscles and joints are moving freely. I can recognise symptoms of anxiety and use my practice to slow things down in my mind and body when it all gets too hectic. Qigong is also a wonderful aid to recovery from illness and surgery.' **Joy**

'I am finding it easier to focus on present tasks, listen more and have a satisfying spiritual connection throughout the day.' **Wendy**

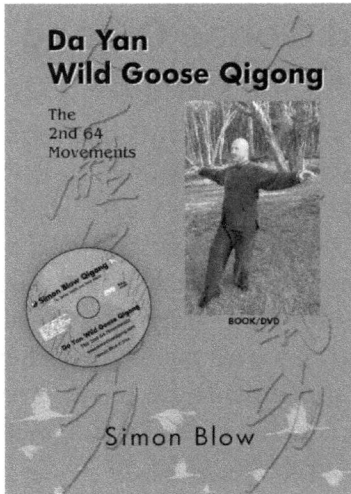

Da Yan Wild Goose Qigong
The second 64 movements

From ancient times, Qigong was an important component of the Chinese medical health system, and developed to help improve people's quality of life. The art of Qigong consists primarily of meditation, relaxation, physical movement, mind-body integration and breathing exercises. When the mind and body come into a state of balance, stress is reduced and there is an increase in health and longevity.

The 2nd 64 movement set of Da Yan Wild Goose Qigong deals primarily with the 'pre-natal body', which refers to the energy we gather from the universe and from our ancestors before birth. Having dredged the channels in the 1st 64 movement set, the 2nd 64 movement set is designed to clear the channels to absorb fresh Qi, expel stale Qi and to restore organ balance. The twisting, stretching, bending and pressing movements produce stronger Qi fields and intensify the circulation through the energy channels. In the 2nd 64 movement set, the Goose embarks on a great journey and flies out from this world to the edge of the Milky Way to pick herbs or gather pre-natal Qi from the core of the universe. It then flies back to this world to share this healing energy with humanity.

'Simon's greatest gift is his ability to make complex concepts so accessible to all people. His teaching is so clear yet so simple and profound that everybody feels included and encouraged to advance further. As a Qigong teacher this is what I hope to achieve in the future.' **Sylvia**

'Qigong has taught me to be more aware of how and what I feel; to listen to my body and to be kinder to myself. My Qigong practice has also given me the confidence to teach with diligence, and to inspire my students. Each day is a wonderful experience; life is good.' **Cherel**

☯ Simon Blow Qigong 偲思
— for better health and inner peace —

To order products or for more information on:

- Regular classes in Sydney for new and continuing students
- Workshops or if you would be interested in helping organise a workshop in your local area
- Residential Qigong and Meditation retreats
- China Qigong Study Tours for students and advanced training
- Talks, corporate classes, training and presentations
- Wholesale enquiries

Please contact:

Simon Blow
PO Box 446
Summer Hill, NSW 2130
Sydney Australia

Ph: +61 (0)2 9559 8153

Web: **www.simonblowqigong.com**

CDs and Book/DVDs can be ordered online and shipped nationally and internationally.

Bibliography

Shanghai Qigong Research Institute. *Gu Yin Liu Zi Jue (Six Healing Sounds)*. Shanghai Scientific and Technical Publishers 2015

Liu TJ, Chen KW et al. (eds) *Chinese Medical Qigong*. London: Singing Dragon. 2010

Ni, Hua-Ching. *Esoteric Tao Teh Ching*. California: Seven Star Communications Group, Inc., 1992

Shou, Yu Liang, Wen Ching Wu. *Qigong Empowerment*. The Way of the Dragon Publishing 1997

Yang, Jwing-Ming. *The Root of Chinese Gigong,* Massachusetts: YMAA Publication Centre, 1997

Blow, Simon. *The Art of Life*. Sydney: Genuine Wisdom Centre, 2010
Blow, Simon. *Absorbing the Essence.* Sydney: Genuine Wisdom Centre, 2010
Blow, Simon. *Restoring Natural Harmony.* Sydney: Genuine Wisdom Centre, 2010
Blow, Simon. *Da Yan Wild Goose Qigong 1st 64 Movements.* Genuine Wisdom Centre, 2014
Blow, Simon. *Da Yan Wild Goose Qigong 2nd 64 Movements.* Genuine Wisdom Centre, 2014

Basic Theory of Traditional Chinese Medicine. China: Publishing House of Shanghai University of Traditional Chinese Medicine, 2002

Liu, Qingshan. *Chinese Fitness*. Massachusetts: YMAA Publication Centre, 1997

Websites

www.wikipedia.org
www.theconsciouslife.com/six-healing-sounds.htm
www.pacificcollege.edu/news/blog/2014/09/05/emotions-and-tradition al-chinese-medicine
www.ichingdao.org/tao/en/level-iv-developing-the-potential/harmoniz ing-the-5-elements
www.acupuncturetoday.com/mpacms/at/article

Meridian charts originally sourced from *Basic Theory of Traditional Chinese Medicine.* China: Publishing House of Shanghai University of Traditional Chinese Medicine, 1988

www.ingramcontent.com/pod-product-compliance
Lightning Source LLC
Chambersburg PA
CBHW081153090426
42736CB00017B/3304